CAMBRIDGE LIBRARY COLLECTION

Books of enduring scholarly value

Women's Writing

The later twentieth century saw a huge wave of academic interest in women's writing, which led to the rediscovery of neglected works from a wide range of genres, periods and languages. Many books that were immensely popular and influential in their own day are now studied again, both for their own sake and for what they reveal about the social, political and cultural conditions of their time. A pioneering resource in this area is Orlando: Women's Writing in the British Isles from the Beginnings to the Present (http://orlando.cambridge.org), which provides entries on authors' lives and writing careers, contextual material, timelines, sets of internal links, and bibliographies. Its editors have made a major contribution to the selection of the works reissued in this series within the Cambridge Library Collection, which focuses on non-fiction publications by women on a wide range of subjects from astronomy to biography, music to political economy, and education to prison reform.

A Garden Diary

Emily Lawless (1845–1913) was a novelist and a prominent figure in the political circles of nineteenth-century Ireland. She was born at Lyons Castle, County Kildare, the eldest daughter of Edward Lawless, third Baron Cloncurry. Although her grandfather had been an Irish patriot with United Irishmen sympathies, Lawless herself remained emphatically opposed to Home Rule. Her novels often explored Ireland's troubled past and present: her first success was *Hurrish* (1886) which was set in Galway during the Land League campaigns and was dedicated to her friend Margaret Oliphant. Although Lawless enjoyed literary success, her personal life was marked by tragedy: her father and two of her sisters committed suicide. Despite her great love for Ireland, Lawless eventually became disillusioned with its politics and moved to England. In this work, Lawless intersperses an account of a year spent tending to her garden in Surrey, with autobiographical and philosophical ruminations. For more information on this author, see http://orlando.cambridge.org/public/svPeople?person_id=lawlem

Cambridge University Press has long been a pioneer in the reissuing of out-of-print titles from its own backlist, producing digital reprints of books that are still sought after by scholars and students but could not be reprinted economically using traditional technology. The Cambridge Library Collection extends this activity to a wider range of books which are still of importance to researchers and professionals, either for the source material they contain, or as landmarks in the history of their academic discipline.

Drawing from the world-renowned collections in the Cambridge University Library, and guided by the advice of experts in each subject area, Cambridge University Press is using state-of-the-art scanning machines in its own Printing House to capture the content of each book selected for inclusion. The files are processed to give a consistently clear, crisp image, and the books finished to the high quality standard for which the Press is recognised around the world. The latest print-on-demand technology ensures that the books will remain available indefinitely, and that orders for single or multiple copies can quickly be supplied.

The Cambridge Library Collection will bring back to life books of enduring scholarly value (including out-of-copyright works originally issued by other publishers) across a wide range of disciplines in the humanities and social sciences and in science and technology.

A Garden Diary

September 1899-September 1900

E MILY L AWLESS

CAMBRIDGE
UNIVERSITY PRESS

CAMBRIDGE UNIVERSITY PRESS

Cambridge, New York, Melbourne, Madrid, Cape Town, Singapore,
São Paolo, Delhi, Dubai, Tokyo, Mexico City

Published in the United States of America by Cambridge University Press, New York

www.cambridge.org
Information on this title: www.cambridge.org/9781108022033

© in this compilation Cambridge University Press 2010

This edition first published 1901
This digitally printed version 2010

ISBN 978-1-108-02203-3 Paperback

A GARDEN DIARY

A GARDEN DIARY

SEPTEMBER 1899—SEPTEMBER 1900

BY

EMILY LAWLESS

METHUEN & CO.
36 ESSEX STREET W.C.
LONDON
1901

To the Garden's chief Owner,
And the Gardener's Friend

A few leaves from this Diary (or something very similar),
have already appeared in *The Garden* and *The Pilot*

A GARDEN DIARY

"A WANDERER is man from his birth," and some of us who have done comparatively little wandering in our own persons, have done our full share of those less palpable divagations which may be performed within a very small compass of the earth's surface, nay even within the radius of a single garden chair.

The gipsy dies hard in many people, and the dreams which have fluttered round our youthful fancy flutter round it still, though youth may have become a memory, and the chances of any serious explorations be reduced to a scarce perceptible minimum. To be a traveller in the real and heroic sense is a very great and a very stirring ambition. To have the hope of wandering far and fruitfully; of bringing home the results of those wanderings; such a hope and such an aspiration is one of the biggest things that can be set before a youthful ambition. With a disregard of probabilities, which, looking back, I can only characterise as magnificent, such

B

an ambition had I, in early days, set before myself.
To be a traveller on the great scale; a visitor
of remote solitudes, and practically untrodden
shores; a discoverer of undescribed forms; a
rifler of Nature's still unrifled treasure-houses—
such was the hope, and such the happy dream.
The words "Unknown to science" floated in
those days before my youthful fancy, and were
to it a shibboleth, as other and more obviously
stimulating words have been to other youthful
brains. Fate has not willed that any such resounding lot should be mine, nor was it, to tell
the truth, particularly likely that it should so will
it. To few of our race has it been given to add,
by even a little, to the knowledge of that race,
and I am not aware that any portion of my own
equipment had particularly marked me out for
this rôle that I had so confidently assigned to
myself.

Luckily we learn to grow down gracefully, as
the sedums and the pennyworts do. A lot that
at ten years old seems unendurably pitiful in its
narrowness, at five times that mature age comes
to be regarded as quite a becoming lot, leaving
room for plenty of easy self-respect, and even for
a spurt or two of the purest and most invigorat-
ing vanity. As that down-growing process ad-
vances we assure ourselves, more and more
confidently, that all the really important, the
vital part of such explorations belongs to us, at

least as much as to the explorers themselves. If we have not thridded Amazonian forests in our own persons with Mr. Bates, or Nicaraguan jungles with Mr. Belt, we know all that those indefatigable travellers have seen, done, discovered, experienced, and only need to take down their books from the shelf to be in the thick of those experiences once more.

So too, with the rest — the botanists, zoologists, paleontologists—greater, as well as less great. With the prince of them all one starts once more upon that immortal *Voyage of the Beagle*, which, besides circumnavigating the world, enables one to accumulate those prodigious stores of observation, destined by-and-by to make one's own name famous to the world's end, and to endow that world itself with one or two practically new departments. With Professor Wallace, one spends years in the Malay Archipelago, till the geography of even the obscurer members of that bewildering group becomes rather more familiar than that of the next parish. With Collingwood one pores over the rock-pools of Chinese seas, which never before reflected human face, or at most that of some shore-haunting Mongolian, uninterested in zoology. With the savants of the *Challenger* one sets forth, with all the pomp of subsidised science, upon a three years' cruise, in search of Globigerinæ, of blind Decapoda, of

Coccospheres, of Rhabdospheres, and other long-titled occupants of abyssmal depths. And if one has been tempted to now and then share the dismay felt by the youthful lieutenant, upon being shown that single teaspoonful of grey slop, as the result of nights of toil, which kept the whole crew of Her Majesty's ship from their bunks, well, one reflected that the wise men probably knew what they were about, and that the teaspoonful in question could hardly be an ordinary teaspoonful. Later, hand in hand one has journeyed with other travellers, some biological, others merely exploratory, or geographical. With Stanley groped for weeks in African forests, and been shot at by un-pleasant little beasts with hands. With Miss North travelled far, yet unweariedly, in search of unknown flowering trees, and other forms of vegetation. With Nansen, until one grew to feel brittle as any icicle, and occasionally almost as callous as one. With Mrs. Bishop, across many seas, and scenes ; and last of all with Miss Kingsley, the only one of these illustrious travellers in whose company I have always felt entirely secure, sure that no dangerous animal —lion, rattlesnake, cobra, shiny tattooed warrior, German trader, or the like—would dare molest me while under her ægis.*

Yes, I have been a great explorer. The earth,

---

* Written in September, 1899. Alas !

and its multifarious contents has lain below my feet, as the Pacific was believed by Keats to have lain below those of Cortez, and if now and then I have been troubled by a passing doubt, a " wild surmise" as to whether all these places really have been seen by my own eyes, I have made haste to put that misgiving aside, as His Majesty King George the Fourth was no doubt in the habit of doing, whenever similar misgivings as to the heroic part played by himself at the Battle of Waterloo crossed the royal mind.

To have been so far, and to have seen so much is good, but to have retained a lowly spirit with it all is even better. To be able, with Alphonse Karr, to set forth on the five hundred and first tour round one's garden, brimming with expectation, and all the certainty of new dis-covery. To be as thrilled over the alternations between the nut-tree walk in winter, and the alpine heights in summer, as ever the family of the Vicar were over those between the blue parlour and the brown. These are the things that really carry a traveller comfortably forward in an easy jog-trot towards his predestined bourne. And if there happen to be a pair of such tra-vellers, a pair of such explorers, and if each of them carries his or her own wallet, or knapsack, and if those two travellers part often, yet often come together again, then what an opening up of budgets takes place! What a retailing of adventures; what a comparison of discoveries; what a vastly extended sense of the round world, and of all the fulness thereof! That there are really great journeys to be performed, great events in life, and great adventures to be met with, I am quite willing to concede; also that there are very small journeyings, very small events, and very small adventures. But the odd thing is that no one seems ever able to decide for one finally and authoritatively which is which!

SEPTEMBER 4, 1899

IT has been wet, and is now fine again, consequently our view of the downs exhibits those tones of vinous purple, shading into indigo, that in moments of patriotic expansion I am apt to call Irish. I do not think it is quite friendly of our neighbours, especially those who live upon the ridge above our heads, to smile so significantly whenever that word "view" happens to slip out, as it did just now, in alluding to our new possession, and its prospects. For what, after all, is a view? The question seems to suggest a reference to the dictionary, and here is Webster, ponderous in brown calf. " View. 1st. Act of seeing, or beholding ; sight ; survey ; examination by the eye. 2nd. That which is looked towards, or kept in sight ; an appearance ; a show." Well, have we not something to look towards, to keep in sight, some appearance, some show? For that matter, so, it may be urged, has the habitant of the "two pair back," or the rustic whose prospect is limited to a survey of his or her neighbours' under

garments,—those "short and simple flannels of the
poor" hung to dry in silhouette against a back
fence.   The truth is it is not at all desirable to
be so haughty.   I will not go so far as to say
that it is unchristian, but it is certainly unbecoming, for are we not all fellow-creatures?   What
if you *can* command seven counties from your
windows?   What if on one particular morning—
to me incredible—you did see three ships cross
Shoreham gap?   What if from your garden chair
you can be regaled by a fantasia of changing
lights and shadows? be lapped into peace upon
summer afternoons, or stirred by the drama of
battle clouds, flung into blackness by a storm?
Well, if you can, be glad of it, but for pity's
sake abstain from bragging!   "Gi' God thanks,
and say no more o' it."   Believe me it is not even
commonly lucky to be so proud, and I speak with
some little authority upon that subject.

For as regards this matter of views, I too have
been haughty to the point of insupportableness.
I too have believed that the possession of wide
prospects argued some peculiar, some ineffable
superiority in myself.   There was a time when
nothing short of an entire ocean, none of your
petty babbling channels, but the whole thundering Atlantic, sufficed for my ambition.   In those
days only upon the largest combination of sea,
sky, mountain ; sea-scape, land-scape, cloud-scape,
did it seem possible adequately to exist.   As for

a mere rustic landscape, as for a confined one, as for a humdrum English one, above all as for a landscape within fifty miles of London, why the mention of such things merely moved my commiseration! Those were the days when to be called upon to leave what is sometimes uncivilly called the ruder island, and to repair, even temporarily, to the more prosperous one, seemed a fall and a degradation hardly to be measured by words. When the contraction of the horizon seemed like a contraction of all life, and of all that made life worth having. When the remembrance that one would have to wake in the morning with no dim blue line to greet one, appeared, to a patriotic, a self-respecting being, to be a wrong and an indignity hardly to be endured without revolt.

Such an attitude is, I now hold, unbecoming in mere mortals, and, like other vaulting ambitions, is apt to precede a fall. The man who starts in life determined to be either Cæsar, or nothing, frequently fails to become Cæsar, whereas with regard to the other alternative, the gods are quite capable of taking him at his word. Happily, life is for most of us a liberal education, and the narrowing of the horizon comes to be endured with a philosophy born of other, and more serious deprivations. It may even be open to question whether any man or woman ever yet was made the better by the possession of a noble view?

That he or she ought to have been made so is quite true, but as a matter of fact, have they? We are moulded out of exceedingly stubborn stuff, and are not often ennobled, I suspect, by the landscapes that surround us, any more than we are by the pursuits we follow, or the names that we carry about with us. Furthermore the essentials of all landscape show a considerable similarity. Much the same sort of clouds and sunshine, much the same sort of nights and days, much the same sort of summers and winters, visit alike the tamest and the wildest of them. Even the more dramatic and exciting fluctuations—snow, and hail, storm, and lightning —exhibit a greater impartiality than might have been expected. The gale that has just unroofed your lordly tower, has equally swept the tiles off our humble porch; in the same way that moralists are fond of assuring us that sickness and sorrow, loss and pain, old age and death, fall equally upon the homes of beggars and of kings.

Never having belonged to the last of these classes, I cannot take it upon me to answer for the discomforts that pertain to it. With regard to the other, though I have often seen myself figuring, or upon the point of figuring, amongst its sad and tattered ranks, the impression has never been a particularly agreeable one, and I prefer, therefore, not to dwell upon it. It was

moreover the subject of landscapes, I think, not
of either kings or beggars, that was under dis-
cussion? But that is the sort of thing that is
always happening! Of all the unsatisfactory
stock to keep, ideas are in my experience the
most unsatisfactory; equally whether they are
winged, or entirely wingless ones. As for a
diary—which, to be of the slightest use, ought to
act as a kind of crow-boy, or goose-girl, to them,
and keep them in order—on the contrary it seems
merely to follow their waddlings and gyrations
with the most foolish, and unnecessary submissive-
ness. The result is that one starts intending to
fill a page with one subject, and before one has
got very far one discovers that in reality one is
filling it up with quite another!

SEPTEMBER 6, 1899.

WE often say to one another that it is impossible that we can have been only two
years and a half in possession here, so greatly
has the scene changed in that time.   Those two
and a half years have done the work of many,
or so it appears to us in our innocent vanity.
Where I am now sitting three years ago stacks
of raw planking rose out of the trampled briers
and bluebells.   The house stood roofed, but
the inside was horrible.   The reign of the
Hammerer had spread to every creature with
ears.   Even in my own little nursery-garden
—chosen in the first instance as the most remote spot—the sound of it went far to extinguish
the nightingales.   Now quietude and a sense
of comparative settlement has stolen over the
scene.   Indoors, when the windows are open,
the birds have it all their own way.   Outdoors
there is still much to be done, much to be
harmonised and regulated, but the first sense
of newness and desecration has, I think, wholly

passed away. This then seems to be an appropriate moment for inaugurating a sort of running commentary upon the garden and its surroundings ; setting forth what the spade has already done, and what the spade has still to do ; what we possess in the way of plants, and what we still visibly lack ; laying bare above all our failures and blunderings in the clearest of colours, with an eye, it is to be hoped, to their rectification. Such a record, honestly kept, must be a highly improving one to look back upon. A man's proper shortcomings, writ out fair in black and white, should contain very edifying reading for that man himself, whatever it might be for anyone else. The worst is that, like other amended sinners, we may come to burn in time with the zeal of the missionary. Not content with our own private flagellations and exhortations, we may sigh to exhort and to flagellate others. Hence doubtless, that vast and increasing host of garden books, which so greatly decorate our bookshelves.

Yet after all a garden is a world in miniature, and, like the world, has a claim to be represented by many minds, surveying it from many sides. If it takes all sorts to make a world, it must take a good many varieties of gardeners to exhaust the subject of gardening. Assuming the said gardener to be of the right sort, naturally we accept his exhortations thankfully.   Assuming him even not to be quite of the right sort—a mere harmless fumbler and bungler—still 'twere rash to assume that he can teach us nothing.   Just as every garden—every real garden, owned by its owner — provides lessons for other garden owners, so even the written equivalent of such gardens, as long as they are genuine ones, not bits of confectionery tossed up to look pretty on tables, may claim the same praise.   So frequently has this of late been brought home to me by experience that, give me only a writer who has faithfully toiled with his own spade, her own trowel, and I am ready to accept a new book at his or her hands every week in the year!

SEPTEMBER 8, 1899

OUR indefatigable old Cuttle has just come to tell me that the new water-lily pond leaks, and that I must send for the bricklayer, in order to upbraid him. I am sometimes asked whether Cuttle is our gardener, and am always rather at a loss what to answer. Hardly, I suppose, seeing that he declines to take much notice of any of our flowers, with the exception of the roses, for which he has a passion. When he came to us three years ago it was merely "on job" from the builders. Our grounds, as grounds, had not then begun to exist. Cuttle stuck the first spade into them then and there, and from that minute their existence began. Since then he has grown to be more and more intimately identified with them, and that to such an extent that I find it difficult now to disentangle the one from the other. Followed by his obedient satellite and shadow, he ranges at large over all that lies between their holly-guarded boundaries. His spade, pick, axe, billhook are masters of all

that come within their reach. Walks, and shrubberies, lawn, and flower-beds began within a
short time of his appearance to emerge as if by
magic out of their primal chaos. Order grew
out of disorder; symmetry to be evolved, and
light to break in upon the very duskiest of our
entanglements. We have a habit of telling our
friends that we ourselves "made" these grounds,
but our part in the process has in reality been
chiefly to sit still, and point our wands. It is
Cuttle, Cuttle alone, who has been their real
creator.

For sheer, beaver-like, apparently instinctive
industry I have never in my life known his equal.
For rooted self-opinionatedness not, I must add,
very often. How he contrives to get through
the amount of work he achieves in the course of
every day, still more how he induces his subordinates to do the same, remains a perennial
marvel to me. Possibly—seeing that my gardening experiences have hitherto lain a long way to
the west of Surrey—my standard as regards
manual labour is not of the highest. That our
Cuttle is a typical Surrey labourer I decline however to believe, though theoretically that, and
nothing loftier, is his status. Early in our acquaintance he discovered my ingenuous surprise
over his prowess. Far from this suggesting to
him that less activity would serve the turn, it
seems to have only spurred him on to fresh and

ever fresh assaults upon my astonishment. That there have now and then been inconveniences in this excess of energy I am free to confess, but that is hardly Cuttle's fault. If, for instance, I remark that such or such new work had better be begun next week, my remark is usually received by him in apparently unheeding silence. Next day however, when I return to the charge, I am told with a smile of pity that the work in question is already done. As I have just hinted this sometimes places me in a position of some little embarrassment. Naturally the work produced at such high pressure rather represents Cuttle's ideal of what it ought to be than mine. To show anything but delighted surprise would be to prove oneself utterly unworthy of such devoted service, and it is only therefore by degrees, and in the most circuitous and disingenuous fashion, that I am able little by little to reinstate my own ideas upon the more or less mutilated ruins of his.

In these early days of September, we stand once more at a new parting of the ways. Within the next six weeks all the essential part of what we hope to see accomplished by next summer must be at all events prepared, or it will be too late. Three chief undertakings at present engage our energies. First there is the new little water-lily pond, and its outer environment of bog. Secondly there is the "glade," which, beginning

C

at the upper portion of the copse near the house,
runs somewhat steeply downhill to its lower end.
Thirdly there is the "long" grass walk, which
passing first along the last named, is eventually
to traverse the whole of the lower portion of the
copse, a distance of some six hundred yards,
crossing as it does so the region of the tallest
bracken, emerging for a while upon a gravel
walk, which skirts the fence of our nursery-
garden, thence, through another stretch of copse,
and between two tall heather banks, into a fresh
tract of birches and sweet chestnuts, till it finally
attains the gate opening out upon the little common at the top.

One somewhat serious problem underlies these,
as indeed all similar little enterprises.   How far,
one asks oneself, may the natural conformation
of any given piece of ground be legitimately modi-
fied?—the most difficult, in my opinion, of the
many small problems which confront the gardener.
The lamentable declivities, the yet more terrible
acclivities, which abound in a certain type of
garden we all know ; objects calculated to bring
the blush of embarrassment to all but a hardened
visitor's cheek.   Like other adornments it is less
their artificiality than their deplorable lack of Art
that so distresses us.   These indeed are sad
warnings, and, remembering them, it is well to
misdoubt our own judgment, and to ask ourselves whether it were not better to abstain

altogether from any attempts at modification, which might lead to results so humiliating and so disastrous?

There are however more encouraging omens. Anyone who has observed how casual, how purely accidental are many of the natural variations of surface which nevertheless give us pleasure, has a right to ask himself whether the spade may not be allowed to produce in a few days what sun, wind, rain, and similar agents can achieve in a few years. I am inclined to think that it may, only it must be a spade with eyes, and if possible with a brain behind it, and both are unusual with spades. In any case wisdom exhorts us to proceed very cautiously and modestly with all such changes. To be sure that in the first place they are called for, and in the second that they will suit with the features of our ground, and the scene in which it is set. Else, if we neglect these precautions, we too may come to swell the ranks of those who have made the very words "landscape gardening" and "landscape gardener" sounds of terror to all discriminating and nature-loving ears.

One of the least unsatisfactory ways of modifying one's ground, and relieving its monotony, is, it seems to me, the "glade." Glades may of course be of many forms, and may suggest many ideas. They may pierce through the dusky heart of a wood, or they may lie nakedly and stonily open to the sky. They may be furnished with trees, with bushes, with heather, with grass, or with alpine plants. On the whole the easiest glade to create, and certainly one of the pleasantest when made, is the grassy one. Even a perfectly level bit of ground can be induced with care to pass by gradations into a grassy glade, though where there is some natural slope the matter is of course very much easier. In that case all that is necessary is to add a sufficiency of earth on either side of the upper part of our incline, leaving the lower to merge by insensible degrees to the natural level. The essential point is not to miss the right moment for the sowing of the grass seed. This month of September is in this soil unquestionably the best month in the year for that purpose. August is apt to be too hot, October may be frosty, while spring sowings are in my experience exceedingly delusive. If the summer that follows them is wet, all goes well. Seeing however that each summer since we came here has been more thirsty than its predecessor, it were hardly the part of prudence to rely upon that.

It has been a satisfaction to us to find that a moderate upturning of the soil does not apparently disturb those inmates of it that we wish to retain. Bluebells and bracken both have their roots at a depth to which the spade in these operations need not penetrate, while to superimposed earth they appear to be quite indifferent. The spring that followed our first operations of this kind bluebells flowered better than usual, as if glad to be freed from some of their troublesome neighbours, especially probably that pest of copses, dog mercury. The introduced bulbs, which now share the ground with them, are mostly of the taller kinds, daffodils predominating, and for these the fact of the soil being all newly upturned is an advantage. Our present plan is that the sides of the glade shall remain permanently uncut, or cut at most once or twice a year, the central, or walking space, being kept regularly mown. The bulbs, being at the sides, will thus not suffer. Moreover the considerable difference of height between mown and unmown grass is bound to give height and emphasis to our little glade. As in the similar case of planting rock gardens, such considerations may seem to some poor devices. Yet upon the successful carrying out of them depends the whole of that "general effect" which is all that such critics probably heed. We are not, after all, Nature's mandatories, and our little slopes are not Alps, or even alpine meadows. If we can attain to so much as a suggestion of the sort of thing we dream of we may rest content.

SEPTEMBER 11, 1899

HERE on the bench beside me is a basket-
ful of plants, not garden ones by any
means, but weeds, mere ugly weeds, detested,
and detestable, which, having pulled up, I was
about to throw away.   And, sitting down for a
moment before doing so, I chanced to turn over
two or three of them in idle mood, and in so
doing have been captured unawares, as I have
often been before, by the wonder, the mystery,
of those ordinary processes of nature, which we
all of us know so remarkably well, and which
we certainly as a rule take such uncommonly
little heed of.

Matthew Arnold has somewhere counselled us
to let our minds dwell upon that great and
inexhaustible word " Life," till we learn to enter
into its meaning.   It was a critic's and a poet's
counsel, but it might still more appropriately
have been a naturalist's or a botanist's.   Life
is indeed one of the unescapable mysteries, a
mystery that expands and grows as we consider

it, even as the hosts of heaven seem to grow
and multiply as they recede before our straining
gaze. For, if we even put aside the more
active animal world, and look merely at the
comparatively placid vegetable one, is it possible
to think of it for a moment without being overwhelmed, as it were stunned, by the vastness
of its effects; by the complexity of its untiring
energy? To take only one of the results of
that energy. It is the plants of the world,
especially those which we are in the habit of
calling its weeds, which constitute its great
restraining forces. The operations of inorganic
nature tend for the most part towards oblitera-
tion; towards the rubbing down of landmarks,
towards the effacing of all individuality in the
landscape. Water, tumbling as snow, hardens
into ice, and rasps away continually at the
surfaces of the mountains. Rivers scrape off,
and carry away with them, every particle of
earth that they meet with on their journey to
the sea. As for the sea, we know that its one
object ever since it came into existence has
been, day by day, and at each returning tide,
to encroach upon, and devour more and more
of the heritage of its brother the earth. Seeing
that the land we live on occupies only about a
third part of the superficies of the globe, it
follows that the whole of what is now dry land
could easily be disposed of below the water;

indeed it has been ascertained that were it thus neatly tucked and tidied away, the level of the ocean would be only altered by less than a hundred feet. It is due mainly to the untiring vigour, to the extraordinary binding power of plants, that this consummation has been averted. Their office has been to hinder a tendency which, even if it had not ended in the submergence of the whole earth, would at least have washed and pared away its irregularities to one deadly monotonous level. Trees and bushes do much in this direction, but it is the little clinging weeds, which as gardeners we detest, and would so gladly annihilate : these crowfoots—why not, by the way, crow*feet ?* — with their crowding roots ; these knotgrasses, these clinging bind-weeds,—it is such as they, backed by sea-spurreys, and bents, and by reeds and rushes innumerable, that do more to keep the waters of the globe in order, and to maintain dry land, than man, with all his dykes, dams, embankments, and such like accumulations, since first he began to strut or to caper over its surface.

But the journey which lies before one's thoughts when once they embark upon this river we call "Life," is indeed too big for them even imagina-tively to attempt. Our boats are so small, and the river so wide, that one soon loses sight of shore. Even if, abandoning these perplexing living things, one falls back upon the mere inorganic forces of the world, what a prodigious amount of energy here too comes into play! Nature everywhere eternally building up, and with apparently no blind hand, but with a most clear, definite, and shaping policy. It is good for us to escape now and then out of our own hot and fussy little rooms, into these larger, cooler spaces; yet, if a wholesome, it cannot be said to be entirely a gratifying experience. For how soon, even in the simplest of such matters, does one arrive, like the people in the *Pilgrim's Progress* at a place called "Stop"? How soon does thought practically cease, and one remains dumb and gasping, like some poor dull beast, in a mere, vacant-eyed daze of wonder? "The mind of man"—it was one who knew what he was talking about that said it—"is an indifferent sort of musical instrument, with a certain range of notes, beyond which, upon both sides, there is an infinitude of silence."

SEPTEMBER 12, 1899

THE Epic of Weeding has still to be written!
It should be undertaken in no light or frolic
vein, but with all the gravity that the subject
demands.   What I should wish to see would be
either a careful scientific treatise by a competent
authority, or, what would perhaps be still better,
a great poem, which, like all the highest poetry,
would go straight to the very soul of the subject,
and leave the votary of it satisfied for ever.   To
the earnest-minded Weeder, most other occupa-
tions seem comparatively subordinate.   Blank is
that day some portion of which has not been
devoted to faithful weeding.   Blank is that night
in which, as he lays his head upon the pillow, he
cannot say to himself that such, or such a piece
of ground has been thoroughly cleared, and will
not require to be done again—for quite a fortnight!
    One disadvantage it certainly has, but then
it is one that it shares with all the other higher,
and more absorbing pursuits.   If inordinately

pursued, it tends to grow upon its votary, until everything else becomes subsidiary. What was originally a virtue, may thus in time come near to growing into a vice. Of this danger I am myself a proof. There have been moments— not many, nevertheless some—when I have found myself sighing for more weeds to conquer. Worse, I have had the greatest difficulty on more than one occasion to keep myself from pouncing upon my neighbour's perfectly private chickweeds and groundsels, which I have happened to catch sight of across a fence!

I notice in myself, and have observed in others, a lamentable lack of accuracy as regards the proper names of weeds. Even some that I know the best, and hate the hardest, I really cannot put any name to. Now this is not as it should be. Everything, however detestable, has a name of its own, and that name ought to be used. You may not like a man, but that is hardly a reason for calling him "What's-his-name," or "Thingamy." It is true that in the West of Ireland it is regarded as a very unsafe thing to mention any of the more malignant powers by their right names. The *Sidh*, for instance, if spoken of by their proper title in-variably fly at you, and do you a mischief. The only way of avoiding this peril is to use some obscure and roundabout designation, which is not their real name at all. I do not know whether the same mode of reasoning has ever been held to apply to weeds. If so, I cannot say that the plan appears to me to answer. At least I can safely swear that I have never called one of them by its proper botanical name in my life, yet they rush in on us from all sides, and persecute us none the less impishly.

There is one particularly diabolical individual, which has clearly marked this garden as its prey, and marches continually to and fro of it like a roaring lion. What its correct name is I shall in all probability never know, though I have carefully cross-examined several botanical works on the subject. It has narrow fleshy leaves; a mass of roots, constructed of equal parts of pin wire and gutta-percha; the meanest of pinky white flowers, and a smell like sour hay. It is not the leaves, the flowers, the roots, or even the smell, that I so much object to. It is the capacity it possesses of flinging out off-shoots of itself to incredible distances, which offshoots no sooner touch ground than they begin to weave a kind of ugly green net over every-thing within reach, enmeshing it all into as dense a mass of leaves and roots as is the parent plant.

Although I am no nearer extirpating it than I was before, since yesterday I have at least been able to name it, a satisfaction which many a poor Speaker must have been thankful for, especially in an age grown too picked and tender to allow

of even the most obdurate obstructor being de-
spatched to either the Tower, or the Block.

It was Cuttle who provided me with that satisfaction, and it is not one of the least of the many
debts that I owe him.

"What can be the name of this thing, I wonder,
Cuttle?" I said, rising exhausted from an effort
to hinder a fresh colony from enmeshing and
strangling a line of " Laurette Messimy " which
had been recently planted upon the top of a
slope.

"I'm not sure as I can tell you its proper
name, ma'am, but about here *we* calls it 'Snaking
Tommy.'"

Admirable Cuttle! " Snaking Tommy " of
course! The instant I heard it I felt convinced
that in that preliminary naming of all plants
and animals performed by Adam in the garden
of Eden, that, and no other, must have been
the name bestowed upon this. It is true some
theologian might assure me that there were no
weeds in the garden of Eden, but that I think is
not particularly likely, because, whether there
were weeds in that garden or not, there are
certainly no theologians in this one. Moreover
we all know that the snake was there, to
everyone's immeasurable discomfort. And if
the snake, why not, let me ask, " Snaking
Tommy "?

HOWEVER it may be in other gardens, seed-sowing, I find, to be the very centre and kernel of this one. The sowing of seeds is apt to be accounted merely a matter of the raising of a due supply of annuals, salpiglossis, nicotiana, lobelia, nemophila, clarkia, bartonia, godetia, "and a long etcetera." With us it is the permanent, the perennial occupants of our flower-beds which must either be grown from seed, or else not grown at all. This fact was early impressed upon our minds, and in a very summary and effectual fashion, such as Nature's fashion of instilling indispensable truths for the most part is.

It was three years ago, and we were a pair of destitute garden-owners. We had however good friends, with large gardens. The connection was perfectly self-evident. Without a moment's hesitation the basket went round. The response was noble. Plants came to us from North, South, East, and West, especially West. Alas for those plants !

They were just what we wanted; they were moved at the right time; they were packed with care; they were not unreasonably long on the road; they arrived to all appearance in excellent health; they were received with all the respect they deserved, and their wants provided for as far as our poor knowledge of those wants enabled us to cater for them. Never were elaborate arrangements less handsomely rewarded. Seasons returned, but never have to us returned those plants so generously bestowed, so hopefully planted. In my private garden-book a list of them still exists, and a very black list it is to refer to. There they stand, as they were written down in all the pride of proprietorship. Unhappily a later entry shows a large round *O* standing out prominently against nearly every one of them. Now a round *O* in that book signifies Death.

From this disaster we arose chastened gardeners. It was determined that no more guileless plants should be brought to such a fate; no more kindly owners exploited for so inadequate a result. Remembering the good, dark, comfortable earth from which most of those plants came; sadly surveying the very different earth to which they had been consigned, the cause of their doom could hardly be called mysterious.

Friendly gardens, unless labouring under our own disabilities, being thus excluded, the question remained how were the flower-beds to get themselves filled? Only one answer to that question has ever presented itself to the professional gardening mind, and that is "Send to the nurseryman."

Now that nurseryman may or may not be an excellent one. Ours, as it happens, may fairly I think be called so. Good or bad he is never a functionary to be approached without deference, at least by those in whose eyes Thrift stands for something in the battle of life. "But common plants are *so* cheap" one is often told. Very likely, they may be; indeed, judging by their catalogues, nurserymen stand habitually astonished before the spectacle of their own moderation. An average herbaceous plant—a lupin, or a larkspur, let us say—costs as a rule about ninepence. It may sink as low as sixpence, or it may rise as high as a shilling. Anybody, it will be argued, can afford sixpence; some people have been known to spend a whole shilling without wincing. A very short walk along any ordinary garden border, calculating as one goes the number of sixpennyworths it would take to fill it, will be found an excellent corrective for such lightheartedness. I made such a calculation myself only the other day, and the result was an eminently sobering one.

Seeds on the other hand are honestly cheap. There are expensive seedsmen, but generally speaking, threepence is the price of a fair-sized packet of the commoner perennials, and sixpence for one of the scarcer kinds. This initial difference is, however, an infinitesimal part of the real one. It is the magnificent possibilities, the vast fecundity of those sixpences, as compared with the others, which is the real point. Not one plant, but dozens of plants, often hundreds of plants, may be the result of a single successful sowing, nor is the time lost by such sowings nearly as great as people seem to imagine.

But the number of plants to be had in the course of a year by this means is only part of the advantage to be gained by it. The great advantage is that by so doing one's plants become acquainted betimes with the qualities of the soil in which they find themselves, and, so getting acquainted, they reconcile themselves to it, as we most of us do reconcile ourselves to any environment, however little naturally to our taste, which has compassed us round from babyhood. To come to details. Alpine plants, though small to look at, are for the most part tolerably dear to buy. If a man, " whatever his sex !" loves his alpines, is determined to have them, has a fairly big alpine garden or border to fill, but will not be at the trouble of rearing them from seed, then I shall be rather sorry for that man's pocket. A few of them —notably the Androsaces—are not amiable in

D

the matter of germination, and these therefore require a mother-plant or two to begin upon. Others, of which the gentians may be taken as a type, are unendurably slow in appearing, though, if a safe place can be found for their seed-box, and it is then forgotten, the time passes! The great majority of alpines, fortunately, will grow perfectly well from seed, even ultra-fastidious ones, such as Silene acaulis, or Ramondia pyrenaica, which for that reason rank high in nurserymen's catalogues, doing perfectly well with care, and, of course, at a fiftieth part of the cost.

Details like these have a sordid ring, and I have to remind myself that it is upon the successful wrestling with them that one's ultimate failure or triumph wholly hinges. Thrift, moreover, is the badge of every proper-minded husbandman, and it is according to the thriftiness of his husbandry that Nature rewards his labours. " But Nature," I hear some caviller exclaim, " Nature is herself the most reckless of spendthrifts. She is the very mother, grandmother, and great-grandmother of extravagance. She squanders her treasures as the rain-clouds squander their raindrops, and tosses her wealth abroad like dust upon the desert air "! True, she does do all this, but I am not aware that she ever specially desired that her children should follow her example. " What are your

poor little savings? your petty extravagancies?"
we might imagine her saying, "that they should
be likened to mine?" Further, by an odd
paradox, it is upon her wastefulness that our
thrift rests most securely. We possess say one
solitary plant of some given kind, and we find
that with that single plant her lavishness has
freely provided us with the material of a
hundred, possibly many hundred others. There
is scarcely a plant we can name that by some
means or another—by division, by layers, by
seeds, by cuttings, or by some other equally
simple variation of the garden craft—may not be
multiplied almost without limit. Truly there is
something staggering about such fecundity, and
the brain of even the strongest gardener might
be expected to whirl as he contemplates it.
Following in imagination the history of almost
any flowering plant—yonder pimpernel astray
on the gravel will do—giving it only time
enough, a fair field, and not too many rivals,
and we shall find that it has gone far towards
peopling every waste place within reach; nay,
if the process could be continued long enough,
by the mere law of its organic existence its
descendants are capable of reddening their entire
native countryside for a dozen miles around.

SEPTEMBER 16, 1899

FEW forms of frailty are more lamentable than vanity, and few variations of vanity have for some time back seemed to me more stamped with puerility than garden vanity. Can anything be imagined more childish, or less worthy of a reasonable human being, than for A or Z to pride themselves on the fact that whereas *Horificus globuratus fl. pl.* flourishes like a weed in their gardens, it entirely refuses to grow in those of B or X, despite the fact that B and X have remade the greater part of their borders, in a spirit of slavish emulation? The same argument applies, even more forcibly, to other details, such as the making of cuttings, or layers, the carrying of tender plants through the winter, the satisfactory growing of vegetables, and so forth; operations which ought to be approached in the largest and most enlightened spirit, and never for a moment made the subject of mere petty self-satisfaction, or of a narrow and arrogant self-laudation.

This point being thoroughly settled, I now proceed to draw out a list of plants grown successfully from seed by ourselves during the last three years; premising that this is only our *first* list, chiefly of rock-plant seedlings, and that I shall have another, much longer, and *much* more important one to draw up when the right time comes!

Alyssum alpestre.
    ,,   montanum.
    ,,   saxatile.
Anemone Blanda.
    ,,   Japonica.
    ,,   fulgens.
Aquilegia alpina.
    ,,   cœrulea.
    ,,   canadensis.
    ,,   Jaeschkaui.
    ,,   vulgaris.
    ,,   vulgaris var. grandiflora alba.
Arenaria montana.
Antirrhinum (various).
Armeria Laucheana.
    ,,   vulgaris.
    ,,   vulgaris var. rosea.
    ,,   vulgaris var. alba.
Aster alpinus.
Aubrietia deltoides.
    ,,   Frœbelli.
    ,,   Leichtlini.
Campanula Carpatica.
    ,,   garganica.

Campanula pumila.
    ,,   turbinata.
    ,,   rotundifolia.
    ,, rotundifolia var. alba.
Cerastium tomentosum.
Cheiranthus alpinus.
Dianthus alpinus.
    ,,   cæsius.
    ,,   cruentus.
    ,,   deltoides.
    ,, deltoides var. albus.
Draba aizoides.
Dryas octopetala.
Erinus alpinus.
Erysimum pumilum.
Erodium Manescavi.
    ,,   macradenium.
Geranium cinereum.
    ,,   sanguineum.
    ,,   striatum.
Gentiana acaulis.
    ,,   verna.
Geum montanum.
Gypsophilla prostrata.
Helianthemum (various)

Heuchera sanguinea.
Ionopsidium acaule (annual).
Linaria alpina.
„   anticaria.
„   cymbalaria.
Linum alpinum.
Lychnis alpina.
Myosotis alpestris.
„   azorica.
Meconopsis cambrica.
Ononis rotundifolia.
Oxalis floribunda.
Phlox amœna ⎫
„   setacea ⎬ cuttings
„   subulata ⎭ easier.
Potentilla nepalenses.
Papaver alpinum.
„   nudicaule.
„   „ var. miniatum.
„   pilosum.
Primula Cashmeriana.

Primula cortusoides.
„   denticulata.
„   japonica.
„   rosea (self-sown),
Ramondia pyrenaica.
Ranunculus montanus.
Saponaria ocymoides.
„   ocymoides var. splendens.
Saxifraga (various; division easier).
Silene acaulis.
„   alpestris.
„   Schafta.
Statice maritima.
„   „ var. carnea.
„   „ var. alba.
Thymus (various; division again easier).
Tunica saxifraga.
Veronica prostrata.
Vesicaria utriculata.

From this list I have carefully omitted all our defeats. Victors I observe, invariably do so!

SEPTEMBER 25, 1899

THE gardener seems to pass amongst his kinsfolk and acquaintance for a rather feeble, but
more or less meditative sort of man. His trade
is held, I perceive, to be productive of some of the
milder forms of philosophy. Like the angler he
enjoys a rather supercilious consideration on that
account from his more violently active brethren.

"You are such a patient fellow," they say.
"You don't care how long you stay pottering
over one small spot. Such quiet ways of going
on would never do for *us!*"

This may be the case, but I cannot say that
I have personally observed, either in myself, or
other gardeners, any tendency to exhibit more
placidity over the cares and crosses of a garden,
than over any of the other cares and crosses of
existence. As for philosophy, a certain sort of
cheap moralising a garden is certainly rather productive of. It sprouts unheeded along the walks,
and may be extracted with greater facility than
most of the weeds. That "life is short"; that

" flesh is grass"; that man groweth up in the spring time, and is cut down in the autumn— such innocent and obvious sprouts of morality as these may certainly be gathered in a good many of its neglected corners. With regard to all the larger and more vital growths of philosophy, I am afraid that they require to be successfully sought for upon wider and more strenuous battlefields.

Lessons of course may be gathered in a garden, as in most other places. For the owner, the most wholesome of these is perhaps that he never really is its owner at all. His garden possesses him—many of us know only too well what it is to be possessed by a garden—but he never, in any true sense of the word, possesses it. He remains one of its appanages, like its rakes or its watering-pots; a trifle more permanent, perhaps, than an annual, but with no claim assuredly to call himself a perennial.

In no garden is this fact more startlingly the case than in those that we have, as we fatuously call it, "made" ourselves. For the owners of such a garden, the precariousness of their tenure is the first thing, I think, that is forced upon their attention. And the reason is simple. In older ones, the reign of the primitive has, to a greater or less extent, ceased, and the reign of the artificial has become the rule. The Wild still flourishes in them, but it has become a mere pariah, a vegetable outcast. Chickweed on the walks, nettles in the shrubbery, daisies in the lawn. "What does this mean? Who gave you leave to be here? Away with you at once, intruders that you are!" that is the habitual standpoint. Now in a new garden, especially a garden that has been won out of the adjacent woodlands, the sense of intrusion is felt—ought to be felt—to be all the other way. It is the so-called owners who are here the trespassers; the unwarrantable intruders; the squatters of a few months', at most of a few years', standing. The bracken, the honeysuckles, the briers, the birds—these are the established proprietors; it is they that can show all the documents of original possession. We may have to eject them, but at least it should be done respectfully; with such compensation for disturbance as would be adjudged in any properly constituted agrarian court in the Universe.

Only yesterday these reflections were forced upon my mind as I found myself, for the third time engaged in a life and death struggle with the bracken, which has once more invaded our newly made flower borders, and threatens to gather their whole contents bodily into its capacious grasp. This is, and always must be, a peculiarly humiliating sort of struggle to be engaged in, and not the less so if one remains temporarily the victor. In the first place, one is deeply conscious of the vandalism of trying to get rid of an object immeasurably more beautiful than any of the plants one thrusts it aside for. In the second place, there is a sense of absurdity and futility, which is strongly upon one all the time. Mrs. Partington, in her efforts at sweeping back the Atlantic Ocean with her broom, was hardly a more conspicuous instance of misplaced energy than such attempts to suppress and control the exuberant green waves, the abounding vitality, of our own magnificent, indomitable bracken.

Even where humiliating struggles like these have ceased to be necessary, how slight an excrescence this whole business that we call ownership really is; how strong, how deeply rooted the state of things which it has momentarily superseded. Let the so-called owner relax his self-assertiveness for ever so short a period; let him and his myrmidons depart for a while upon their travels, and how swiftly the whole fabric rushes remorselessly back to its original condition. And why not? What can be more absolutely to be expected? Nor need we even stop at the garden, the farm, the house, or any similar chattel. Even ourselves, sophisticated little creatures though we be, in how many ways we remain the accessories, rather than the masters, of our environment? For a time, especially in towns, we manage to conceal this truth from ourselves. We pretend that we have remodelled

matters to our liking; that Nature has become
our follower; that our law, not hers, runs through
the planet; that we set the tune, and that she
merely plays it.

Oh rash, and hurrying ignorance! Put the
holder of so untenable a doctrine alone, for
ever so short a time, especially in the winter, in
the solitary depths of the country, and how soon
a perception of his or her own utter transitoriness
will begin to break through the thinly formed
crust of the new, and the superimposed. Let him
lift his garden latch, and step out beyond it into
the open country. Let him saunter alone in the
woods after dusk. Let him walk across the
solitary, blackened heather. Let him look down
upon the floods, lace-making over the lowlands.
Let him—without taking so much trouble as this
—merely lean out of his window after dusk, amid
the thickening shadows, and he must be of a
remarkably unimpressionable turn of mind if the
sense of his own shadowiness, his own inherent
transitoriness, is not the clearest, strongest, and
most convincing of all his sensations.

Thus vanity provides its own solution, and
the little inflated soul is driven into puncturing
its own proudly swelling balloon. We discover
—sometimes with no little dismay—that it is
not alone in our flower-beds that the wild and
the tame, the temporary and the permanent,
the real and the artificial, meet, jostle, and rub

shoulders together. Sir Primitive is a remark-ably difficult person to escape from. His blood still courses unheeded through our own veins, and he is as much a part of ourselves as he is a part of the most sophisticated of our plants or our animals. We may imagine that we have left him behind us, and outgrown his teachings, and the very next day something will occur to show us that he is at our elbows all the time, as strong, as fresh, and as absolutely unaffected by any little modern innovations as he ever was.

SEPTEMBER 26, 1899

YET, although undoubtedly our ancestor, Sir
Primitive stands a good way back on the
family tree, and other influences have grown
up since his time to disturb his teachings. The
fear of becoming too tidy, for instance, does not
at first sight seem to be a very reasonable fear.
It has not been imputed to many people as a
failing, especially to those who happen to have
been born to the westward of St. George's
Channel! Nevertheless there are moments when
a wild passion for tidiness, a perfect thirst and
craving for order, seems to sweep across the
soul like a wave; when everything else that
one habitually cares for is flung back, and overwhelmed before it, even as the hosts of Pharaoh
were flung back, and overwhelmed before the
cold, subduing waters of the Red Sea.

We are all the children of our age; there
is no getting over that fact; heirs of a hardly
won civilisation, let us call ourselves Wild Wilful-
ness, or any other law-defying name, as much as

we please. Yearning to show that our spirits
are above all trammels, that we are as free
as the birds in the air, we nevertheless all
sit in identical armchairs, eat the food the
cooks provide us, and in most other respects
exhibit about as much originality as so many
stair-rods.

It is only necessary to consider what happens
every day of the week in the garden to perceive that this is the case. We have adopted
the most independent line possible ; we have
vowed that *our* gardens shall be natural ones, or
nothing. We adore flowery wildernesses, we
declare. We want our plants to grow as Nature
intended them to do, and not as the hireling
gardener does. We intend to put a limit to the
eternal bolstering up of our soil with all sorts
of extraneous elements ; above all we will have
nothing to say to the clipping of our shrubs
into unreal shapes, nor yet to the planting of
our bulbs, and other flowering plants into lines,
squares, and parallelograms, but all shall be a
melting and a blending of one harmonious form
into another ; every detail, as far as the eye
can reach, being subordinated to the larger
and more important spirit of the landscape as
a whole.

So we say ! And yet, after the flag of freedom has been thus ostentatiously raised, what
happens ? As often as not we find ourselves,

by the logic of facts, and by the realities of the situation, forced slowly to retreat, as other and equally eminent strategists have been forced before us. A flowery wilderness is delightful, but unless its owner is content with the flowers that grow in it by nature, or a few, very cautious additions, his flowery wilderness is apt after a time to become a wilderness, minus the flowers. Then perhaps a reaction sets in. A sense of failure gradually overtakes the too ardent amateur. The reins of authority drop more and more listlessly from his hands; until at last he lets them fall altogether, and, with a smile of kindly pity, the momentarily dispossessed professional once more resumes full, and henceforth undivided sway.

From so humiliating a finale may all the kindly divinities that watch over gardens deliver ourselves! Nevertheless there have been moments when such a fate has seemed to draw near, and even to look one in the eyes. Only three days ago I was engaged in that breathless struggle with the bracken. For the last two, aided by Cuttle and his assistant, I have been fighting ankle-deep against a perfect forest of couch-grass, which had practically overwhelmed the whole of our nursery-garden, helped rather than hindered by the fence, with which we had innocently hoped to keep back, not alone rabbits, but every other trespasser.

Worse than the conduct of the couch-grass, because of a certain personal element in it, has been the conduct of the rose-campion. Now I have been exceedingly kind to that rose-campion. Again and again I have intervened to rescue it, when it was on the point of being rooted out, and consigned to the dust-heap. Only last spring I carried its roots by hundreds with my own hands, and re-established them in a special reservation ground, where they might spread unmolested over a good half-acre or so of copse. What has been the result? They have indeed clothed their allotted space, but, not content with this, they have burst like a horde of Ojibeway Indians, or some such aborigines, out of their reservation, across the frontiers of civilisation, sending out myriads of seedlings ahead of them, like a flight of skirmishers, and are now nearly as numerous collectively, and far more luxuriant individually, in the nursery, than they are in the copse itself!

Incidents like these wound one, and are more trying for that reason to the amateur gardener than to the professional one, who probably regards them as only to be expected. I am far from saying that they constitute a sufficient reason for surrender, but they certainly seem to need the aid of a higher quality than mere secular doggedness, to enable one to grapple with them as one ought. It is moreover such

occurrences as these that produce that extraordinary thirst for order, that very unlooked-for
passion for tidiness, which I just now noted.
After a day or two passed in such struggles as
these one begins to understand the pride of the
colonist in pure, speckless Ugliness; in beauti-
fully clean, naked earth, varied by straight lines
of split-wood fences, or the like. I have not
as yet reached that point myself, and am glad
to feel that I can still tolerate Nature. All the
same a sort of nurseryman's attitude towards
everything tainted with wildness is fast gaining
upon me, and unless I can check both it, and
this overweening love of tidiness while there is
time, I plainly foresee that there will shortly
be nothing else left!

E

" FOUNTAINS ; they are a great beauty and refreshment, but pools mar all, and make the garden unwholesome, full of flies and frogs."

For two persons who have just been at some pains to establish a pool in their grounds, this is a hard saying! That the judgment has much to support it, apart from the weight of its utterer, I cannot deny. At the same time a better case can, I think, be made out for the culprits than may appear at first sight. Fountains in a copse, be they never so limpid, never so sparkling, would be stamped with an unendurable stamp of artificiality. Pools on the other hand, though there are certainly not many in these copses of ours, are at all events not inconceivable. In the present case we flatter ourselves that the particular spot we have selected for our pool was intended by Nature to contain one, and nothing but the incurable aridity of these dry hillsides hindered her from carrying out that intention. Where every drop of water has to be watched over like hid treasure, it may be doubted whether the amount that we can afford to have trickling through it in summer will suffice to hinder the water in it from becoming yellow, brown, or green. That is a point however which remains for future discovery. Our main preoccupation at present rests with the planting of the edges of our pool, especially with the clothing of the bank which, rising to the north of it, will absorb most of the midday sun, and will require therefore the most attention.

In its present condition a good deal of that bank looks bare to desperation, yet I strongly suspect that summer will prove it to have the reverse fault of being crowded with a dense, and inextricably entangled mass of vegetation. Fortunately half its present inhabitants, being biennials, will depart after the first season, when, the prospect clearing, the permanent inhabitants will stand forth confest and visible.

Omitting this temporary part of its furniture, I will jot the others down as they stand, which will enable us to see what we have, and also to form a better idea of what we still lack.

First and foremost a kindly gift; two large clumps of Arundo donax, easily supreme anywhere as pond-side decoration, the more so, as they quickly attain to their full size. No other plant of the reedy order, not even excepting a bamboo, gives quite the same impression of vigorous, of almost insolent energy as does this one. It adapts itself moreover perfectly to our sandy soil, and so long as one sees that it receives a reasonable amount of moisture, seems to ask for little else. Next follow two or three plants of Arundinaria japonica, and below these again Arundinaria, or Bambusa palmata, skirting the edge of the pond, and passing on into the so-called bog. This last came from Kildare, where it has established itself, and run practically wild along the edge of a lake. Here it seems to do its growing more slowly, but the plants are spreading, and I think promise fairly. Below the other bamboos, but above palmata come two large plants of Astilbe rivularis, placed so that their arching leaves will overhang their lower neighbours, and all but touch the water. Next, turning the corner of the pond, come various low-growing bushes. Berberis Darwini below, with the faithful Aquifolium, and the taller stenophylla above, ending in a fringe of bog-myrtle, and of Rodgersia podophylla, among which some Solomon's seal are now barely discernible. After these come a few plants of Hemerocallis, both fulva and flava, which need continual dividing in the borders, but seem to flower well, and give no further trouble so long as they are within reach of an occasional splash. Acanthuses appear to be in the same position, the difference between their growth in wet and dry soil being extraordinary ; indeed when one remembers how they abound in Spain and Italy, one fails to understand the limp and desolated aspect they see fit to assume here, under a very much more moderate dispensation of drought.

Next follows Funkia Sieboldi. Funkias are all meritorious plants, but Sieboldi, to my mind, towers head and shoulders above the rest. Apart from the beauty of the flower, its grey-green, almost iridescent foliage is like no other leaf that grows, and when the two are combined the result is High art, art at its best point. Such praise is, however, merely impertinent. It is more pertinent to say that the whole genus, but especially Sieboldi, belong to that very limited category of plants that are at once fit for the most orthodox of beds or borders, while at the same time they are free enough, and independent-looking enough, not to seem ridiculous in a bit of pure " wildness " such as this little pond-side purports to be. This is far from being a common virtue. One only needs to run over such words as "Hollyhock," " Begonia," "Pelargonium," to perceive in a moment what would be intolerable outside of a more or less stiff parterre. It is not so much a question of beauty, as of fitness and adaptability, perhaps also of freedom from certain set associations, which, having once rooted themselves in our minds, make it impossible for us ever to rearrange our impressions, and recast them in a new form. This however is a digression. To go on with my list.

Upon the actual edge of the pond we are at this moment planting some two dozen varieties of Iris Kæmpferi. These have recently come from Haarlem, and being still new-comers, have their destiny ahead of them. The common yellow iris, best and handsomest of all native, water-edge plants, had only to be transplanted, as it was already flourishing close at hand. As a successor to it comes Ranunculus Lingua, another indispensable native, but one that requires sharp watching; its capabilities as a coloniser being unlimited, the long, pink-tipped suckers pushing forward into the water at a rate that would soon turn any limited space of it into a mere jungle of triumphant buttercups.

In the part of the bank which, sloping rather quickly away, inclines towards the "glade," come various low-growing shrubs, which carry the line down to the region of heather, which in its turn brings it to the level of the grass. The tallest of these,—rather too tall for the place,—is Viburnum opulus, common beside many a Surrey pond, but not nearly enough grown in gardens, as the best of amateur gardeners has recently reminded us. Its cultivated relation, Viburnum plicatum, is just beyond it, placed there, not because there is the slightest occasion for its being upon the water's edge, simply because it happens to be one of those plants that never seem quite happy unless they have abundance of space to move about in, the long shoots, laden with blossom, having a wonderful power of reaching out to distances that at first sight seem to be quite beyond their grasp. Another plant of which the same may be said is Hydrangea paniculata. So far ours have spent their existence dully in tubs, the idea being that they required winter protection. Judging by some that were experimented upon last winter this seems to be a mistake, and I propose to try a few here, by way of successors to the foregoing, with which their equally industrious sprays seem to possess a sort of kinship.

Our grassy "glade" being now all but reached the remaining corner of the bank has been filled with various grass-leaved flowering plants, which seemed to come in appropriately. Of these the largest is Libertia formosa, green all the year round, and in summer bristling with white, iris-like flowers, and, by way of plant-fellow to it, Sisyrinchium Bermudianum (Plague upon these polysyllabic dog-latinists!), one of the friendliest of little plants that ever pined for a decent English name. Put it where one will—on a bank, in a bog, in a flower-bed—it seems equally happy and appropriate ; always compact, yet

increasing as rapidly as any weed ; above all continually in flower, even, so I noticed last winter,
in the middle of frost and snow, and when its
leaves were so brittle that they snapped when
they were touched, like any icicle.

My list seems to be already stretching to a
tolerable length, yet there are plenty of things
that have not yet found their way into it. Here
is Bocconia cordata, for instance, impossible to
do without in such a spot. Here are the spider-
worts, both blue and white. Here are various
spiræas, chiefly low - growing ones, such as
" Anthony Waterer " and palmata, the latter only
happy in a more or less damp place. In the
peat-filled hollow beyond quite a little crowd of
claimants rise up for notice. A good many of
these are now only satisfactory in the retrospect.
Of such are Primula japonica, and Primula rosea,
sorry-looking tufts of brown shreds, with no new
leaves as yet showing. Cypripedium spectabile
is in the same plight, but Hellonias bullata is
still green, Gentiana asclepiadea has a flower or
two showing, Lobelia cardinalis, both the older
and newer varieties, look red and happy, and
Schizostylis coccinea promises fairly, though it
never behaves with us quite as it ought to do,
and as I have known it behave in kindlier soils.

Turning to the region of mere dryness, three
or four rough stone steps, and a ridiculous
little ridge, lead towards the azalea corner.

Here cistuses of various kinds have their home, and, being fairly sheltered, do well, though several require remembering in the winter. I find the same to be the case here with regard to the rosemaries, especially the younger plants, as they grow older they seem to harden. Lavenders fortunately are safe everywhere, in all weathers, and the same may be said of Skimmia japonica and Fortunei, two of the most satisfactory of small winter-flowering shrubs. These with a few tufts of Andromeda floribunda, and a small jungle of alpine rhododendron, bring us up to the azalea corner.

All these plants, especially the more recently planted ones, will need pretty constant looking after during the next year or so, but once that crucial period of their existence is over, it is my hope—possibly only my delusion—that they will learn so to arrange their affairs as merely to require the sort of attention that is necessary to see that they do not overcrowd one another, or—what is more serious—become invaded by wild neighbours, rose-campions, and the like, swarming in upon them to the point of suffocation. The safest way of avoiding this is undoubtedly to cover the ground with low, carpeting growths, which will remain green nearly all the year round, and at the same time not make too severe a demand upon the soil. The number of such kindly little evergreens, or semi-evergreens is a constant surprise when one comes to collect them, and the fact that there should be so many speaks volumes for a climate that we are none of us ever weary of abusing. Apart from absolute rock-plants, nearly all of which are evergreen, there are a number of others, which rarely or never lose their leaves, and whose presence saves banks and hollows like these from the reproach of bareness, and further takes away —certainly ought to take away—all excuses for visitations from that Tool of the Destroyer, the pitchfork. Of such plants none are better than certain campanulas, including our own hair-bells, both the blue and the white. Wood - sorrels again are excellent in a shady place, or, for a sunnier one, there is their energetic cousin Oxalis floribunda, in this soil the most undaunted of colonisers, growing all the winter. "Creeping Jenny" again, and "Blue-eyed Mary," delightful things with delightful names, will cover as much space as they are allowed to do. Of the more easily grown forget-me-nots there are at least four kinds—palustris, for planting close to the water, or in it ; dissitiflora, happy all the summer, so long as it gets a little shade ; sylvatica and alpestris, growing anywhere, and everywhere. Epimediums, again, are excellent, though apt to get a little rusty in the winter. So is Tellina grandiflora, an unwisely named plant, since its strength lies, not in its flowers, but its leaves.

Thymes, too, are always available ; likewise
potentillas, erysimums, and veronicas, though
these last may seem to be trenching upon the
rock-plant region. Then, if we want larger
growths, are there not all the megaseas, which
may be torn in pieces two or three times a year,
if we like? Of low-growing shrubs, such as
Euonymus radicans, the various creeping coton-
easters, the savin, Gaultheria shallon, and others,
there is no lack. Yet another, and one of the
best of them all, Cornus canadensis, a true shrub,
and an evergreen one, although no larger than
a wild wood-strawberry.

But I find myself growing breathless, and the
list of such kindly " carpeters " is in reality only
begun. Flinging down woodruffs, wild pansies,
foam-flowers, sedums, mossy saxifrages, wald-
steinias, and periwinkles, as one might out of
a basket, I will only now delay to find room for
a few rock-pinks, particularly for these four—
cæsius, cruentus, atro-rubens, and deltoides,—all
of which may be sown broadcast in the spring,
and all of which, especially the last, may be
trusted to hold their own against any but the
biggest and most ferocious of natives.

We have been honest caterers for our clients,
as far as preparation went, and my hope, I may
say my ideal, is that they will henceforward be
content with receiving merely surface nourishment from time to time, and will neither look for

or need that eternal process of renewal, and as a consequence of disorganisation, which is the bane, though I am willing to admit the unavoidable bane, of nearly every flower-bed and border.

Ideals are odd things, and this one of mine seems, even as I write it down, about as ridiculous and puny an ideal as any forlorn idealist was ever driven into making a boast of! Such as it is, however, I cling to it tenaciously. After all what does it mean? Written out a little large it means repose of mind, and a freedom from the strain of change; it even means a certain sense of finality, and that at a very sensitive spot in one's small environment.

To a greater or less extent we all sigh for finality. Nobody has ever attained to it, that I have heard of, and not many people would perhaps relish it if they could do so. None the less it remains, something haunting; a dimly descried presence, to us vaguely desirable. To sit at ease under their own vines; to be at rest in their own shaded places, has from the earliest days flattered the imaginations of men, busy and idle ones alike. Dawdlers in sunny places, and haunters of gardens like ourselves are naturally assigned to the second of these categories. Since we have to support the reproach of idleness, let us at least then take heed that we secure the comfort of it. If Leisure is an acquaintance of ours he is an

acquaintance of so few people nowadays, that
we had better make the most of him. Now
fuss the good man detests, and change, merely
for change's sake, is undoubtedly one of the
very worst forms of fuss. Like every other
pursuit and following, horticulture no doubt
has its battlefields, and those who go out upon
them must expect charge and countercharge,
rapid assault and varying vicissitude, like other
heroes upon other battlefields. For me such
combats, I am free to confess, have not even
a vicarious charm ; Peace being the only deity
to whom I would willingly raise even the
smallest of garden altars. With other out-of-
door conditions we all aver that it is their
stability, their adorable unchangeableness, which
lends them in our eyes their most persistent
charm. Why then are we not to look for the
same charm in our gardens, which after all come
nearest home ? That it is a charm easy of attain-
ment I were loth to asseverate, but that seems
hardly a reason for not endeavouring to attain
to it. It is in this direction at all events that
my own private plottings and plannings propose
to turn. If I must moil and delve ; if I must
plant, dig, and contrive now, it is with the fixed
and fond determination of before long sitting
resolutely down, and doing absolutely nothing !

OCTOBER 27, 1899

WHO dare forecast even his nearest future?
These last four weeks have been so charged
with anxiety—not only, or even chiefly, war anxieties—that I have not made so much as a single
entry in this diary. In fact there has been nothing
to record. The poor little garden; its flowers;
its weeds; the copse surrounding it; the entire
mise-en-scène, with all the quips and jests which
in sunnier hours it gives rise to, seems to have
vanished bodily. It is as though the whole thing,
erstwhile not without its own little importance, had
dwindled to the size of one of those infinitesimal
specks, which one sometimes sees in feverish
dreams; specks so dim and small, so well-nigh
invisible, that one wonders how in the first place
one ever discovered them, and why, having done
so, one should take the trouble of trying to keep
them in sight. That being the case it is as well
that I am leaving home to-morrow for several
weeks, and, since I shall be chiefly in London,
have a good excuse for leaving the garden diary,

like the garden itself, behind me. Possibly, by
the time I return to them, the old, now submerged,
landmarks may have risen once more to the surface, or I may have grown a little better used to
this changed landscape ; seeing that we all have
to get used to every variety of landscape ; every
admixture of weather; every cruel, blinding storm;
every rain-washed shore, or bitter, wreck-strewn
sea, which meets us in this very odd journey that
we call our lives.

CHRISTMAS-DAY, 1899

THERE was a slight sprinkling of snow this morning, yet the garden looks exceedingly black. Save for a scarce discernible white line here and there, everything in it seems stiff, and hard, and black as iron; crumpled iron leaves against an iron floor. Black is the livery, not alone of sorrow, but of dismay, so that the garden does very well just now to wear it. There are moments in the individual life, moments, so it appears, even in an entire nation's life, when the ordinary scheme of things seems to dissolve and change; when all the familiar landmarks for the time being melt away, and disappear under our eyes.

Standing here, staring blankly out of the window, I feel myself for the moment a sort of embodiment of all the other, vacant-eyed starers out of windows, up and down over the face of the country this Christmas morning. How many of them there must be! How many must be staring down at the dull ground, and telling themselves they will never care to walk in, or to look at their gardens again. It may not be an actual garden, but at least it will be a figurative one ; some special plot of happiness ; some quarter-acre of habitual enjoyment. I hope, indeed I feel sure, that in the great majority of cases they will sooner or later enjoy it again. Father Time is at bottom a kindly creature, kindlier than when in trouble we are inclined to believe him to be. For the moment however the idea seems unrealisable, and would scarcely be welcome if it were realised.

For hardly-pressed humanity there is, I believe, only one really satisfactory way of dealing with misfortune, which is—to refuse to believe in it! That is, I find, the method that our excellent Cuttle in the garden has adopted with regard to most of the recent events in South Africa. Anything exceptionally disagreeable, especially anything that has to do with the surrender of Englishmen, no matter under what circumstances, he simply declines to believe in. It is not that he is ignorant. He reads his paper diligently ; he knows everything that is in it, but he refuses to accept more of the contents than he considers proper. When, a few weeks ago, the first of our Natal mishaps occurred, and the number of English prisoners captured was posted up in the village hall, Cuttle informed me the next morning that he had seen it, but that there wasn't a word of truth in it! I demurred, but he stuck to his

F

guns steadily. It was the same last Monday, when I saw him for the first time after our two most recent misfortunes, that of the Modder and the Tugela.

"This is bad news, Cuttle," I said, as we met outside the greenhouse.

"Well ma'am, they do try to make it out to be baddish, but I wouldn't believe it, if I was you."

"But it is in all the papers, Cuttle."

"Very likely it is ma'am, but what of that? I don't hold with none of those papers. They must be a-stuffing themselves out with something."

"But I'm afraid the generals admit it themselves."

"Excuse me ma'am, but that's just where you're making a great mistake. We don't know nothing about what the generals admit. All we know is that the papers *say* they admit it, which is a very different story. Mark my words, you'll find that it'll turn out to be some of their muddlings. Just you mark my words for it, that's how it is."

I said meekly "I hope so, Cuttle," and walked away, for really I had not the heart to try and shake his incredulity. Not that I imagine I could have done so had I tried. That good, homespun garment of British pride in which he had wrapped himself was proof against any assaults that I could have brought to bear upon it. I wish with all my heart that he would lend us each a piece of it. We want it badly. Pray heaven and all its saints that we may none of us ever need it much worse than we do this Christmas-day, 1899!

.   .   .   .   .

CHRISTMAS-DAY, 4 P.M.

SINCE luncheon I have been to see a neighbour, in the vague hope that some fresh war news might have arrived this morning. There was none of course, and I walked home again between banks of withered bracken and trailing bramble, under the big tree-hollies, glistening all over their surfaces with a thousand reminders of Christmas, and of its gifts. England is so big, and old, and sensible that she does not generally care about Christmas presents, but there is one present that, I take it, she would dearly like to have to-day. Shiploads of holly, forests of mistletoe are hers for the asking, but that one little leaf of victor's laurel that she wants so badly, that she would so gladly pin upon that broad breast of hers, this, it seems, is denied her. It may come to-morrow. It *must*, we all, not alone Cuttle, feel convinced, come before long, but it will not come in time for her Christmas-box.

What an odd convention it is, when one thinks of it, that habit of embodying a country in an individual! Considered seriously the whole contention is absurd. To talk of a nation as a person is to talk sheer nonsense. If one handles the idea a little it tumbles to pieces in one's fingers. The fiction of unity resolves itself into a mere vortex of atoms, all moving in different ways, and moreover with a different general drift in each successive generation. As a matter of fact I doubt whether Englishmen, who are nothing if not practical, ever do think of their own country as an individual, unless one of them happens to be called upon to design a coin or a cartoon. The whole idea is extraneous, a survival from classical days, and the lumbering absurdities which are now and then dragged about the streets only go to prove how far from the genius of the people such representations really are.

Perhaps it is because I am not English that I find myself falling so readily into the trick. There was a time,—not a very recent one— when I thought of England habitually in that light, and in the most truculent fashion possible. In my eyes she stood visibly out as the Great Bully, the Supreme Tyrant, red with the blood of Ireland and Irish heroes. It was always *she* and *her* then ; indeed it was only by keeping up the fiction of an incarnate Saxondom that

indignation could be retained at the proper
boiling point. To turn from the past to the
present was to spoil the whole effect. In place
of War, Famine, Massacre, one only got dull
political controversies, or equally dull agrarian
disturbances. For the Raleighs, the Sydneys,
the Straffords, the Cromwells, — vast impressive figures, large and lurid — only a group
of rather harassed gentlemen, " well-meaning
English officials," painfully endeavouring to steer
their way so as to offend everyone as little
as possible. Yes, I had quite a respectable
capacity for hatred in those days, and England
—that historic England of which I knew absolutely nothing—enjoyed the greater part of it.
Especially, I remember, that I used to gloat over
the notion of some day or other a great national
HUMILIATION befalling her—a Sedan, a
Moscow — I hardly knew what ; retribution at
all events in some very visible and dramatic
form. With what glee I used to picture her
standing helplessly before the nations ; without
a friend or an ally to turn to ; naked and
ashamed ; crushed bleeding to the earth, as she
had so often crushed Ireland ; a mark for every
wagging head——

Well, well, thus we play the fool, and the
spirits of the wise sit in the clouds and mock
us! Here am I walking home along an English
lane, and almost wringing my hands in despair

because such a very mild and colourless version
of those old cherished dreams has befallen mine
ancient enemy!

CHRISTMAS-DAY, 6 P.M.

I FORGOT to record quite an unlooked-for
little pleasure which befell me on my way
home this afternoon; one of those little incidents
which are nothing in themselves, yet which mean
much to us, and never more so than when life is
going ill.

I had got as far as the grassy entrance to our
copse when a sudden dazzling gleam of sunlight
shot across it, sweeping over the fields beyond,
and away up to the top of the downs.   Though
the day had been fairly fine for the time of
year, the expectation of so dramatic a finale to
it had never for a moment crossed my mind,
and I stood gazing about me almost as if something had happened; feeling in fact as if something desirable and unlooked for *had* happened.

The yellow oak scrub—withered but not leafless—glowed with a sudden russet splendour.
Upon the little garden wall the terra-cotta pots
shone with a momentary reminiscence of that
Italy where they were born and baked.   The
air seemed to tingle; the tall birches glistened,
one sheen of feathery silver up to their tiniest

towering twigs. It was a kindly thought of whichever divinity sent that most unexpected and satisfactory beam to cheer this particular day. It did not last long of course, and the gloom of a winter's night has followed quickly. For all that Christmas 1899 will never seem quite so dark, never so absolutely despairing in the retrospect, as it would have done without that last benevolent gleam at eventide.

JANUARY 3, 1900

THE satisfactions of intercourse are apt to be overrated, yet there are times when they are certainly not without their uses. Living for the moment alone—if anyone can be said to be alone who possesses a few good neighbours, and one kind dog—I find myself in an oddly dualistic condition of mind. In bodily presence I am here at H——, engaged in sundry important avocations. I am path making; copse cutting; plant protecting; I am even bricks-and-mortar superintending in a small way. To my own private consciousness I am really engaged in quite another set of preoccupations, and a very long way from these green downs, and rustling oak copses of ours. The experience does not pretend to be particularly original, seeing that a large number of other people's experience would probably just now bear it out. Solitude however emphasises these sort of odd dualities, and endows them with an air of greater distinction. Are mortals better and wiser, or worse and more foolish when they are alone?

The wisdom of the ages has hitherto declined to answer that question, a fact which probably proves its wisdom. Better or not, one thing is at least certain, and that is that they are extremely different. " Men descend to meet," says Emerson, and he may be right. I am inclined myself however to think that that profundity, that peculiar mental greatness of which, like others, I am perfectly conscious when I am alone, is less a solid than a gaseous greatness ; a sort of exaltation, dependent for the most part upon the fact of there being no one to contradict me. We are all of us at all times microcosms, but never are we so completely microcosms as when we are quite by ourselves. Then we seem to swell into a perfectly multitudinous host, all the members of which exhibit a singular unanimity, and moreover a touching desire to endorse our own views, however often these may contradict one another !

Like many other honest-minded civilians, my thoughts have of late been considerably taken up with schemes of amateur strategy. The plans of campaign that I have formulated in the course of the last two months would have puzzled Von Moltke, and might even have gone far to surprise Napoleon ! If I have not forwarded any of them to our Generals in South Africa it has been mainly because I felt that it might be kinder to allow them to go on in their own way without any assistance of mine. I heard lately of someone, by the way, who actually had telegraphed out her recommendations to Sir Redvers Buller.   As the story reached me the telegram took this form : "Please try to relieve Ladysmith." I hope for the credit of human nature that the tale is true, but if so there is a simple innocence about this form of admonition of which I fear that I should have been personally quite incapable. My own ideas, my own forms of suggestion, are entirely different.   They are large, nay grandiose, and moreover they are extremely intricate.   As I walk about over these lanes and downs I see strategical possibilities in all directions, which cause me to thrill over the magnitude of my own conceptions.

Towards evening, especially, the sense of what might be,—of what, for aught anyone can say to the contrary, still may be,—rises almost palpably; a beckoning ghostly phantom of the Great Coming Invasion.   Dorking — that scene of crushing British disaster — is not far off; were I to clamber up the opposite ridge I should be looking down on it.   Moreover, between one landscape and another the difference becomes much less when all detail is reduced to one vast blur. I have a friendly knoll upon which I sometimes take my stand towards sunset hour, and from which I have of late conjured up Biggarsbergs, inaccessible and kopje-covered as heart could desire.   It is true that the enemy holding them is absolutely invisible, but then so he probably would be in any case. Evening has moreover in my experience an odd power of loosening the tie of the actual. The mind seems to be less fixed to its shell than in the earlier, and more garish hours of the day. As the shadows lengthen stronger and stronger becomes the impression that the world is after all but a small place, and that the scenes that one is thinking of are nearly, if not quite, as close as those that one is actually looking at. Thought flits over the wave-crests between this and South Africa more lightly than one of Mother Carey's chickens, and alights dry-shod upon the veldt. One is amongst them. One is standing in the midst of them. One can see, literally all but see, that tattered, sunburnt, rather dilapidated-looking host—friends, cousins, kinsfolk; countrymen and fellow-subjects at all events. How odd you all look, dear friends, and yet how familiar! Big English frames, shrewd Scotch faces, tender, devil-may-care Irish hearts. Surely one knows you? Surely you are very near to us, disguise yourselves as you may? The setting may be new, the remoteness considerable, but neither setting nor remoteness can hinder one from feeling at home in the midst of you!

JANUARY 6, 1900

" BULLETS—The air was a sieve of them. — They beat upon the boulders like a million hammers. They tore the turf like a harrow!"

These three lines came out of a recent number of the *Daily Mail*, and they describe Elandslaagte. Is it, I wonder, because Literature is so much more familiar to me than War that I seem to require the aid of the one in order to bring home to me the reality of the other? These three lines are certainly literature, literature of the impressionist kind, which, if not the best in the abstract, is at any rate the best for such a purpose. Trying to put oneself into the position of such a bystander as the writer of them, I am able to fancy that if the bullets came thick enough they really *might* seem to tear the turf like a harrow. In what way exactly the air could be said to be a sieve of them, I am not clear, yet the phrase seems to live, and therefore to carry its own justification. As it happens I was out yesterday in a rather exceptionally imposing hail-storm. It was so dry that there was no occasion to hurry, and I stood still for a while to study effects. The stones, as they pattered and rattled round me, might—danger apart—have quite served as a suggestion of the other sort of rattling and pattering. Looking at them dispassionately I inquired of myself, "Would one run?" and Truth—there being no one else present—promptly replied, "Madly!" So, save for the grace of acquired training, I take it would nearly everybody. My hail bullets seemed to be in a prodigious hurry, and were being prodigally, if not very scientifically, directed by marksmen concealed somewhere above Leith hill. They hissed, they danced, they ricochetted off the trees, they bespattered the ground in all directions in a very businesslike and realistic fashion. There was a good deal of snow still lying unmelted in corners, and into that snow the new-comers as they fell cut deep little pits, and disappeared from sight in an instant. Elsewhere they drove in white flocks over the ground, hardly melting at all. They were not quite so large as carrots, as someone assured me that he had once seen hailstones, but they were certainly as large as fair-sized gooseberries. Through such a furious hail—only appropriately black—

the famous Bagarrah cavalry rode to their deaths last September year. Through such a hail, as thick, as fierce, as brutally indifferent, who that one knows, that one cares for, may not be riding or walking to-day?

JANUARY 8, 1900

WE have been enveloped all this morning in a cloud of smoke, not exactly battle-smoke, but nearly as thick, perhaps, in these days of smokeless powder, rather thicker. Our inde-fatigable Cuttle has decreed that we must at all costs get rid of those mountains of garden rub-bish, which seem to be for ever accumulating. Hence this smoke! Never in my life did I see such volumes! They rolled in blackish blue columns all about our leafless copse, till towards the afternoon, a wind getting up, they were swept finally westward, across the downs, somewhere in the direction of Guildford.

Personally I like the smell, acrid though it undoubtedly is. The pile itself is moreover the nearest approach one ever gets in these de-generate days to a bonfire, for which I still retain the most infantile affection, and which never seems to be so familiar, or so endearing, as upon the afternoon of a winter's day. Who can explain those incredibly remote, yet at the same time perfectly definite feelings of association, of which we are all at times more or less aware? Why should certain perfectly commonplace things awaken dreams, reminiscences, suggestions; whereas others, every bit equally qualified to do so, find us blank, and indifferent? Of all such aids to impersonal memory, commend me to an out-of-door fire! The wild, keen smell of it. The red eye of flame, blinking at one out of the heap. The sleepy rolls of smoke, tumbling about, and making one's eyes water. The sudden "crick, crick, crackle" of a snapping twig, travelling sharply through the frosty air. All these separately, or the whole combined, bring with them trains of association that have been accumulating very much longer, or I am much mistaken, than the course of any one single lifetime. Reminiscences, who can tell, of that remote day when the human hearth was for the most part not an indoor, but an out-of-door one?

A friend and neighbour of ours has recently improved upon such casual burnings by having what may be called a permanent bonfire in her grounds, and I wonder more people who love their gardens, and spend whole winters in the country, do not adopt the plan. In one respect it is certainly an inferior bonfire, for its main constituents are, not leaves and sticks, but anthracite coal. To make amends, it burns merrily away night and day, only needing to

be replenished, I am assured, once in twenty-
four hours. Her garden lies in the heart of a
big pinewood, and the fire has its home in an
open lodge or gazebo, supported by larch poles,
without door or window, but made possible to
sit in in cold weather, by being match-boarded
upon two sides, the south and south-east sides
alone being widely open. Until one has actually
tried, it is difficult to believe how comfortable
one can be in such a spot even on a very frosty
evening, both feet extended to the blaze, and
a rug tucked round one to keep off stray
draughts. As daylight wanes the red glow
increases, lighting up the big pine trunks, and
awakening in one's mind vagrant suggestions
of camp fires, and forest settlements, while at
other times it has the practical advantage of
making many garden operations possible which,
without such a speedy refuge to fly to, would
in this chill-evoking climate of ours scarce be
practicable.

It is odd what minute deviations from the
everyday stir the mind, and help it to shake
off that crust of routine, which it ought to be
the aim of all of us to get rid of. In these
days too, one is thankful to anything that gives
a stir to existence, apart from the weary newspapers. It is, I think, one of the few merits
of winter that spots, at other times tame to
flatness, seem in fierce, or exceptionally cold

G

weather to revert to an older, and a wilder condition.   Snow admittedly recreates everything;
our most familiar paths and shrubberies, nay our
very stable runnels, growing quite arctic and
hyperborean-looking under its disguise.   Apart
from snow, the same impression is produced
by any really strong atmospheric variation.
Crackling grass, and glittering ice-bound trees,
awaken one set of suggestions.   Roaring winds,
a drenched earth, and inky clouds tumbling
wildly over the sky, arouse quite others.   Even
objects inside the garden, plants that have been
perhaps put there by one's own hands; clumps
say, of bamboos and reedy grasses—Arundo
donax or the like—assume suddenly new, and
slightly savage aspects when one sees them
sweeping to and fro, or buckling like so many
fishing rods under the lash of a sudden tempest.
The commonplace is not really unescapable,
though it often seems as though it were.
There are wider, freer notes, which only need
awakening to stir, and thrill us with their
presence.   The imagination leaps to meet them,
and feels them to be its right.   For we are all
heirs to a large inheritance, though we are apt,
as a rule, to be forgetful of the fact.

TWO kindly days in a desperately grim winter have had the effect of reawakening in one's mind half-forgotten thrillings ; thrillings after long grass, and green shadows ; after a thousand eye-caressing tints ; after the pure, delicious life and companionship of flowers. There are times when all this seems rather to pain than to please. When the persistency of such perishable things appears but an added wrong, but an additional unkindness. Why should these last, and other, and higher ones, *not* last? we demand ; one of those questions which, seeing that they can never be answered, it were as well, perhaps, that they should remain permanently unasked.

Walking briskly along the lanes this morning, with a determination to think only of what lay immediately below my eyes, I have been struck afresh, as often before, by the capabilities of beauty possessed even by the poorest plots of ground ; plots which, far from having been intentionally beautified, have been stripped, on the contrary, for utilitarian reasons of such beauty as Nature had originally endowed them with. Yet, under the influence of a little kindly sunshine, how they still gleam, those poor plots; how the few green things left in them manage to prink themselves out, and to respond genially to that genial greeting! "And is it not slightly discreditable," I reflected, "that we, who call ourselves gardeners, and have deliberately taken in hand similar, often much better plots, specially with an eye to beautifying them, should again and again completely fail in doing so; should again and again spend thought, time, money, and the sweat of the brow—chiefly of other people's brows—and all that they should, as often as not, be rather worse at the end than at the beginning?"

The truth is that this business of "beautifying," into which many of us have recklessly plunged, is a very much more difficult and a very much more delicate operation than we are prepared to admit. To the truly discerning, the truly nature-loving eye, the smallest scrap of plant-producing ground, the homeliest corner of earth—"long heath, brown furze, anything" —has potentialities of beauty and interest which even the best gardener rarely develops as they might, and ought to be developed. It is not merely that individually our powers are weak, our taste poor, our ignorance great, our imagination defective, but that over and above all this we have in most cases not the faintest idea of what we are aiming at. With no clear vision of what we propose ultimately to produce, how in the name of reason can we hope to produce it, or anything else worth having?

The cause of the mischance in nine cases out of ten lies in the fact that we attempt too much. Our original combination may have been good, but we want to make it still better. Our gold gets overgilt ; our lilies are painted till they almost cease to be lilies at all, and the result is failure all along the line. This sounds the reverse of encouraging, but I am not sure but what it is in some respects better that it should be so. I suspect that all gardeners—professionals and amateurs, experts and gropers, —are just now rather in a state of flux and indecision. Two chief schools hold the field, and are in some respects mutually destructive of one another. There is the school which avows itself the faithful, not to say the servile, follower and imitator of Nature, and there is the school that proposes to itself to improve upon her. The tendency of the first is to develop a good deal of picturesque disorder, a pleasant, rather easy-going sense of repose, and possibly some want of definite form and colour. The tendency of the second, or rather of its members, is to regard the garden as a battle - ground; colour, size, brilliancy, height, as so many tests of their own personal victory, and every plant, species and hybrid alike, as objects for them to shape and manipulate at their own good pleasure.

Will these two divergent schools ultimately combine into one harmonious whole? Will the over-strenuous science of the second strengthen and reform the airy, somewhat weed-encouraging grace of the first? Will the aspiration after beauty of the one, in time relax the utilitarian tension of the other? These are questions which must be left to be resolved in the still unplumbed future. Possibly the gardener of the twenty-first or twenty-second century may be able to reply to them!

Pending that desirable, but still rather remote, contingency, I have left the lanes, and returned homeward, and am now looking down at our own somewhat chaotic little garden, with its small brown beds, each edged with a neat white frost-frill. Poor little garden! I have felt so oblivious of it of late that a certain compunction comes over me as I look at it. After all, gratitude for such good things as have come in one's way is an undoubted part of decent living, and the most practical way of showing that gratitude is to make the best of them. Well, the year is still young; there will be time enough for fulfilling that, and every other small social obligation in

the course of it.   Eleven and a half months!
What unknown things have you got hidden
away?   What secrets, as yet unguessed at
by any of us, do you keep concealed behind
those picturesque, and friendly-sounding names
of yours?

JANUARY 20, 1900

THE wind this morning was excruciatingly cold, with a hungry whistle, that belied the pale sunrays, which were doing their best to redeem the situation. On such a morning the good gardener's thoughts, even before going out, fly to the younger and weaklier amongst his plants, and his imagination towards devising new shelters, and, if possible, more efficient ones. Creepers are, as a rule, easily protected; either there is a wall, against which mats can be laid, or, at worst, some post that they can be fastened to. It is shrubs in the open that present the greatest difficulty; nightcaps of sacking, or tents of matting not adding to the picturesqueness even of a winter garden.

Our more recently planted rhododendrons look anything but happy, and I have just been begging Cuttle to bestow a good shovelful of nourishment about the roots of each of them. It is not protection that they need, for they are hardy enough, but they sicken in this thin, dry soil,

which seems to reach them through their two-
foot blanket of peat.

Even when well grown and long established,
rhododendrons hardly seem to me to be quite
the ideal thing for these rustling oak copses of
ours. We plant them, partly for the sake of
their colour in its season, partly because we need
evergreens, and the common ponticum is one
of the best of evergreens, but they seem to me
to remain exotics, and not altogether happy
ones. There are two distinct varieties of scenery
with both of which rhododendrons consort
magnificently. One is heavy, boggy ground,
deep, dark, and oozy, under large trees, into
the recesses of which they can settle, spreading out in all directions, re-rooting themselves as they choose in the black earth; their
flowers catching the divided sunrays, and turning every hollow place into a pool of colour.
Another, and a yet more ideal place is a steep
hillside, provided that it is furnished with
boulders, and provided that the said boulders
are not of limestone. There is one such hillside above the Bay of Dublin which I find it
difficult to believe might not be able to hold its
own, even though confronted with any similar
extent of ground amongst the Himalayas themselves. It begins as a ravine, rising out of
a rather thin wood. As one mounts the
ravine opens, and the trees fall back. The

boulders, with which the slopes are covered, rise higher and higher, and larger and larger, till they tower into the air over one's head, perfect monoliths.   In and out, above, behind, and between them grow the rhododendrons, in their flowering season an absolute feast of colour, the sort of thing that in a cultivated age pilgrimages will be formed to venerate.   To see them in such a place is to get a new impression of the possibilities of heroic gardening. One's eyes are caught, one's whole mind and spirit is swept away upon a tide of colour; the grey micaceous granite of the ravine, the heather looking down over its top, the long blue river of sky, even the sea and its ships, seeming to be merely so many adjuncts and accessories of the central picture.

Such conditions are not to be found every day in the week, or in everybody's back garden. We have to work out our own redemption, each of us as we best can, with such materials as the Fates have lent us.   Happily, as regards natural conditions, here in West Surrey, the garden-lover, whatever other difficulties he may have to contend with, has much to be grateful for.   Thanks to its blessed unproductiveness, the harrow has literally in many cases never passed over its soil; its very weeds being mostly those of Nature's own introduction, not imported ones.   Her handiwork is still plainly visible on every side. She looks up at him out of the bracken with an aspect not very different from what she wore at the Prime, and if he wishes to spoil her—well, he has to do it for himself! This to many excellent gardeners would seem a poor compensation for a sadly unproductive soil, and a deplorable lack of summer moisture. There are others, however, to whom a certain sense of indwelling peace, a certain feeling of underlying harmony, are the first of all requirements. Now both of these are more easily *found* than made.

FEBRUARY 5, 1900

NOT to devote an indefinite number of hours to the reading of war news; to eschew the luxury of idle hands, less on account of Dr. Watts' reasons against it, as on account of more personal ones, which have taught me to reprobate the practice. Here are a couple of respectable resolutions for a bitterly cold February morning. "Books, and work, and healthful play"! Could a more commendable little programme be invented? or one that might be followed with greater advantage by many of us who only exhibit our superiority by laughing at it?

Into which of the two latter categories gardening is to be ranged I am not quite clear; it depends, I should say, upon the number of rose-campions, "Snaking Tommys" and the like, that are to be found in the garden in question. Winter is supposed to be a time of year which gives comparatively little scope to the energies of the amateur gardener. If so, then in this respect, if in no other, I am in luck's way this

winter, for there is abundance to be done here ;
work moreover which must either be attended
to now, or else not done at all. With such
weather as we have of late had there is no
margin either for dawdling. To-day seems to
be an off day with the frost fiend's gang, and
we must try, therefore, to push our own work
forward before they are back upon us in renewed
strength. By the look of the sky, and the
general feeling of things, it is evident that they
are only just round the corner, and collecting
themselves for a fresh assault. As I crossed the
open end of the "glade" just now the wind
met me with an edge, cruel and cutting as spite,
or hatred. A few aconites and snowdrops are
pushing out their flower-tips, but it is a mere bit
of gallant bravado upon their part. By night
the stars, seen through any uncurtained window,
seem to wink at one derisively, and winter is
still at the very top of its strength.

" AT the very top of its strength ! "   Cold as it
has been of late, I hardly expected to find
no garden left when I got up to-day ! So it is
however.   Late last night everything seemed
normal.   This morning our little Dutch garden
has vanished utterly ; swept out of existence as
though it had never existed.   From centre
to margin—beds, borders, walks, red walls,
everything—the entire little depression has been
covered with a uniform white blanket, effacing it
completely, and restoring the landscape to what
it was before man, woman, or measuring tapes
arrived to trouble it.   For the plants this new
state of things is an improvement, but how
about our work ?   Behold us suddenly reduced
to a state of deadlock ; all our various little
activities brought to an absolute standstill.   The
paths that were being cut through the copse ;
the ground that was being got ready for grass-
sowing ; the flower-beds that had to be clipped
into the right shape ; the heather that was being

brought from a distant common, where it could
be cut discreetly ; the entire bustle of the garden
has been brought to a condition of arrest. Into
the middle of our fussy little rhythm Nature has
dropped her own imperious full-stop. Against
that full-stop there is no appeal. In vain one
protests that one is really in a great hurry ;
that unless these flower-beds are made, unless
yonder piece of ground is got ready for grass-
sowing, March will be upon us, and close at its
heels, April ; that the spring is coming on, and
that we *must* get our work done. To this
remonstrance Nature merely opens her eyes with
a mildly sarcastic air, and replies, " Must you ? "
It is the case of the old woman of the nursery
tale over again, who *had* to get her pig over the
stile in order to give her old man his supper.
In that case she did, after many repulses, find
a complacent beast, I think, who undertook the
task. The right spring was touched ; the spell
broken, and the whole state of deadlock dis-
solved at once. How we are to obtain so
desirable a dissolution I have yet to learn. I
see no spring to touch ; no bird, beast, or
element that could be appealed to with the
slightest hope of success. The sky, iron-grey,
with vicious, inky streaks across it, does not
seem promising ; neither does the wind, which
keeps to its beloved north-east. The earth is
invisible, consequently is for the moment out

of reckoning; while as for the birds and beasts, they are much more disposed to turn to us for help, than to make any friendly propositions the other way.

It may be mere vanity upon my part, but it always seems to me that small birds recognise their heavy, wingless, two-legged kinsfolk with less difficulty during this sort of weather than at any other time of the year. The fact that one bribes them to such recognition by vulgar doles of breadcrumbs may have something to say to the matter, but I fancy that I read a distinctly kindlier expression in their eyes. They glance at us with an air of comparative condescension. They perceive that we share their own helplessness; that we are not so very different from themselves, only bigger and stupider. For instance, I have been publicly snubbed this whole winter by the tomtits. Under the eye and to the knowledge of the entire garden I set up a large post, hung over with cocoa-nuts for their convenience. Some of these cocoa-nuts were sawn into slices, others, more artfully, into rings, and I pleased myself by believing that they would sit and swing in them, as they pecked an unfamiliar, but not unpalatable meal. Will it be believed that not one tomtit has deigned to touch those cocoa-nuts? They have hopped to and fro on the boughs almost within peck of them, yet never so much as tried to ascertain whether they were eatable or not. They preferred, in fact, not to do so ; in *their* family, they practically sent me word, they never ate victuals that had not been selected by themselves ; other people might do so, and they had heard that sparrows were less particular, but it had never been *their* custom. I felt—as anyone would feel under the circumstances! To-day for the first time, thanks to the friendly connivance of the snow, this fastidiousness has broken down. With elation I perceive my disdainful blue neighbours, not only pecking at, but actually sitting and swinging in the long-despised brown rings. I am trying to bear my triumph meekly, and am helped towards doing so by reminding myself of the well-known fact that in times of stress and famine social distinctions are apt to break down. I shall have to wait till the weather relaxes to see whether this amiability is anything more than a truce, born of the hour of trouble, and not intended to last beyond it.

We are apt to talk as if the hyperborean conditions were no concern of ours, yet, as Alphonse Karr long ago remarked, we have only to sit still to find that these, and most other extremes of climate have come round to us. It was the tropical or sub-tropical regions of the globe that not long ago were good enough to send us specimens of their weather, as enterprising tradespeople enclose samples of their goods in envelopes.

H

There were many days last summer—to be accurate, I believe, there were forty-three—when it was by no means necessary to go to the Sahara in order to ascertain what a condition of almost unendurable drought could be like. For the present I feel that these two samples will suffice me. I cannot, unfortunately, return them, since I do not know their sender's address, but I feel under no obligation to charter either camels or whale - boats, in order to go and make their acquaintance upon a larger scale.

As for the mere ferocity and killing powers of Nature we are not without a taste of her capacity even in that respect. Apart from the wild creatures, which have to look out for themselves, she exacts in weather like this a pretty stiff list of victims from the old, the weakly, and the very young. My energetic chow Mongo insisted upon my taking him for a late run through the snow this afternoon, and, as we stood for a moment near the stile, there came up a melancholy little chorus of bleatings from some sheepfold in the valley below us. I peered over into the white darkness, but could see nothing ; Mongo licked his lips, and I earnestly trust that he was not thinking of mutton. It may be mere weakness on my part, but I have always felt glad that in my various communings with the good green earth I have stopped short at the garden, the wood, the bog, the hillside, and have never once

stepped into the paddock or the farmyard. In
reading lately Mr. Rider Haggard's *Farmer's
Year*, I found my pleasure a good deal interfered
with by the eternal and the detestable apparition
of the butcher! Whenever the small lambs, that
frisked so delicately, were beginning to grow
plump; whenever certain Irish bullocks, whose
vicissitudes one followed, were pronounced to be
not improving as they ought; even when the old
milch cow, who had given so much good milk,
and had brought so many calves into the world,
began to flag—always there was that abominable
apparition in a smeared apron waiting for them
close at hand, or peering in sinister fashion from
round a corner. No, whatever other functionary
I might be willing to share my pursuits with,
assuredly I could never consent to share them
with Mr. Bones! The objection may be merely
sentimental, but so are most of our likings and
dislikings merely sentimental. As for these green
clients of ours, it is true that they do die pretty
frequently upon our hands, and the fact is, no
doubt, very distressing, the more so as in nine
cases out of ten we are aware that it is entirely
our own fault. In their case there are at least no
heartrending cries or groans, heard or unheard.
They go to their own place in peace, wafted as it
were by slow music towards the gentlest of dis-
solutions. While as for ourselves, if we are their
murderers, well, we manage to hold up our heads,

and take particular care never to allude to the subject. On the contrary, we put on an air of extra cheerfulness, and make haste to plant something else!

FEBRUARY 10, 1900

THAT resolution about the war and its news-papers I still feel to have been the right one. Unfortunately, like many excellent resolutions, it has only one drawback, which is that it is impossible to keep to it! The situation has grown too strained; it clutches at one like a demon; it rides one all day like some waking nightmare. In vain I assure myself that the proper attitude for all non-combatants is one of absolute patience. That it becomes us just now to study patience, as we might study one of the fine arts; to learn, that is to say, either to go about our own concerns, or else to wait till we are told—as we might be at the end of an operation—"All over!" "All well!" This, I have no doubt, is the proper and patriotic atti-tude, only how is it to be attained? or who is sufficient for such placidity? It is not so many days since I opened my paper at eight o'clock in the morning, and the message heliographed by Sir George White to Sir Redvers Buller sprang to meet my eye. "Very hard pressed" and immediately below it the comment—"Here the light failed"!

"Here the light failed!" That seems indeed to be the summary of the whole situation. One question at least we are all forced to ask, if not with our lips, at least inwardly. What of Lady-smith? Will it; can it now be reached? and if not what is the alternative? Such thoughts are gadflies, and would drive the tamest mad. Restlessness gets possession of one. The thirst for news, more news, ever more, and more, becomes a possession ; one that is no sooner slaked than it revives afresh. My particular garden boy has been turned into a mere newspaper boy, and spends his whole days running downhill to the station, on the bare chance of another paper having come in, or of someone having seen someone, who may possibly know something.

Has it often happened I wonder in the history of a country that this sort of external and public news—the news of the street and of the newspaper—becomes to each individual his own absolutely private news ; news that for the moment seems to supersede even the acutest personal grief ; news that makes the tears start, the pulses throb, the heart, at apprehension of what may be going to happen, literally stand still from fear? The thought of Ladysmith, it is no exaggeration to say, amounts to an agony. One feels it in one's very bones. Fear of what its fate may be is the last thought at night, and one awakens to remember it with a sensation of despair which would be ridiculous were it not so real.

For the odd part of it is that not a single creature near and dear to me is shut up within those walls. My interest in it is therefore a purely external one, the interest of a citizen, nothing more. If we—myself, and others in the like case—feel it thus acutely, how must the situation stand to-day, to-morrow, all these pitiless, interminable days, to some?

FEBRUARY 12, 1900

I HAD occasion to go to Guildford yesterday despite the weather, and met in the train our eminent horticultural acquaintance, Mr. R. P. We have always a good deal to say to one another on the subject of our respective gardens, although his is a long-established and renowned one, ours such a callow young thing that it is hardly fit as yet to be called a garden at all. On this occasion, seeing that he was coming from London, my first remark was not a horticultural one.

" Is there anything fresh ? " I asked. " News seems so often to come in just after the morning papers are out."

" Fresh ? Oh, you mean about the war ? No, I think not. Everybody seems to be pretty sick over the whole business. I saw Sir F. J. the day before yesterday, and he was very much in the dumps about it. He says the Tommies out there don't like it one bit. That they have got their tails regularly between their legs, and I'm sure *I* don't wonder."

"How dare he!—I mean I don't believe a
word of that!" I exclaimed. "Anything else
I am willing to believe, but not that. We have
got our tails between our legs here at home if
you like; I am quite ready to admit that. But
they! Never!"

"Well, I don't know. I only tell you what
I hear. They have had a baddish time, you
must remember. Stormberg and all that!—quite
enough to give anyone the jumps, *I* should say.
Of course it has been kept out of the papers.
In the papers the Tommies always figure as
heroes. Is Anemone Blanda in flower with
you yet?"—this with a sudden rise of anima-
tion.

"Anemone Blanda?" I repeated, feeling slightly
confused by the rapidity of the transition. "Yes.
At least no. I think not—I haven't looked
lately."

"It is with me! Sixteen tufts in full flower—
beauties! I shelter them a bit of course, but
only to save them from getting knocked about.
You never saw such a colour as they are!
Yours were the pale blue ones, weren't they?
I know there's a lot of that sort in the trade
that are sold as Anemone Blanda, but they're
not the right Blanda at all. Mine are as blue
as, oh, as blue as—blue paint."

"We have numbers of bulbs at present in
flower," I said severely. "Scillas and chino-

doxas, and daffodils, and tulips, and Iris Alata, and many others."

"Ah, potted bulbs. They're poor sort of things generally, don't you think? Some people, I believe, like them though."

"We have Cyclamen Coum in flower out of doors," I added; garden vanity, or more probably deflected ill-humour, arousing in me a sudden spirit of violent horticultural rivalry.

"Oh, you have, have you?"—this in a tone of somewhat enhanced respect. "Don't you shelter it at all?"

"Not in the least!" I replied contemptuously. "We grow it out in the copse; on the stones; in all directions. It is a perfect weed with us. No weather seems to make the slightest difference."

I am really surprised that I did not assert that we had Orchids and Bougainvillæas growing out of doors in the snow! It is probable that I should have done so in another five minutes, for irritation sometimes takes the oddest forms. Luckily for my veracity our roads just then diverged; my horticultural acquaintance getting out at the next station, and I continuing on my way to Guildford.

I don't think I have ever in my life felt more ruffled, more thoroughly exasperated than I was by that most uncalled-for remark about the Tommies. Had they been all individually my sons or my nephews I doubt if I could have felt more insulted! I adore my garden, and yield to no one in my estimation of its supreme importance as a topic; still there are moments when even horticulture must learn to bow its head; when the reputation of one's Flag rises to a higher place in one's estimation than even the reputation of one's flower-beds. "Anemone Blanda!" I repeated several times to myself in the course of the afternoon, and each time with a stronger feeling of exasperation. "*Anemone Blanda*, indeed!"

FEBRUARY 13, 1900

IF what lies beyond the next few weeks could be suddenly laid open to us, what should we see? It is, I am aware, rank cowardice upon my part, but if by merely ruffling over the blank pages of this diary which I hold in my hand I could in an instant find out, I know that I should refuse to do so. The same feeling has beset me before now, but hitherto always with regard to personal matters; never, so far as I can remember, with regard to public ones. Three weeks! It is not a very long time. Only a few more crocuses and scillas will be out in our little Dutch garden; only a few more oaks and chestnuts cut in the copse, yet within that time the fate of Ladysmith must be decided. Should help fail to reach it—and it may well prove impossible—what shall we see? what will the world see? what will our various enemies see? Only two alternatives appear to be open: an unbelievable surrender, and an only too easily believable slaughter. That last of course is the

central thought, the unendurable one; the vision
that hangs before one's eyes day and night.
Death upon those iron hills; death without the
possibility of accomplishing anything; death under
the most unendurable of conditions; shot helplessly, like the furred or the feathered beasts of
a *battue*. I write it down deliberately, in the
hope of thereby getting rid of it, for it haunts
one unendurably. With that perversity, which
makes us all at times our own most ingenious
torturer, my mind revolves continually around
the disaster before it comes, and fills up every
detail with the most diabolical distinctness. "Fall
of Ladysmith! Fall of Ladysmith! Destruction
of the garrison!" It seems to reverberate along
the roads; it presents itself upon every village
hoarding, as a friend of mine saw it several times
this winter upon those of the Paris boulevards.
Before I open my paper in the morning it seems
to be hidden under the folds, ready like an asp
to spring out and poison me. At night I fall
asleep to the thought of it, and in my dreams it
performs wild and Weirtz-like antics, projecting
itself in and out of them with all that monstrous
reduplication which the besetting idea has a
way of achieving for itself, when the brain
that originated it is nominally asleep, and at
peace.

LONDON, FEBRUARY 16, 1900

GOD be thanked! God be thanked! one of them, at least, is safe. Kimberley has been relieved, and the others, assuredly the others will follow? This leap from a midnight of gloom to a midday of joy has been almost too great; life, even for the most placid, has become too breathless, too crowded; let me pause a moment and recapitulate. I came to London upon Saint Valentine's day, the 14th; S. S. being on her way south; circumstances delayed her a day, and in that day all this happened. We had gone to see a friend; she left me to take a turn in the Park; in a few minutes she returned breathlessly; she had met a park-keeper and he had told her the news. Five minutes more we were both in the park; had caught the same inspired park-keeper, and had fallen upon him simultaneously.

"Is it true? How do you know? Who told you?"

" Quite true ma'am. Quite true ladies. You'll find it written up at the War Office."

" But how? Where did they get in from? The enemy were right across; so——"

"Well ladies, as I understand it were like this. General French was sent north, and he fetched a big circuit as it were so. And——"

With our umbrellas we drew a hasty but effectual scheme of attack upon the park gravel, then hurried away from our gold-braided informant in the direction of Pall Mall.

Oddly enough St. James's Palace did not appear to be in the least irradiated by the intelligence! its grim old face remained as unresponsive, and as dirty as usual. Everything else however had caught the glamour. It shone upon the cabs, or at any rate upon their cabbies; it lit up the sea of mud; it seemed to float along the pavements scoured by a recent shower. Men were coming out of the clubs in groups, talking loudly; everyone talked loudly; not an acquaintance was in sight, yet they seemed to be all acquaintances; more than acquaintances, friends, dear friends; we looked benignantly at them, and they looked benignantly back at us. In London; in St. James' Street! Tall or short, stiff or pompous, young or old, it was all one; they were brothers; brothers in a common joy, brothers in a common relief from an all but maddening dread. To smile for no reason in some perfectly decorous stranger's face seemed to be the most usual, the most natural behaviour. Safe! Safe! It was a chime, one which needed no joy bells to make it sound louder. Surely for us at least it was worth the strain, worth the long suspense, the almost hopeless anxiety for this? And Ladysmith? and Mafeking? The turn has come; the tide has changed! We shall shortly hear the same news of them. We shall be rejoicing over both of them to-morrow!

SURREY, FEBRUARY 26, 1900

THERE is a little tapestry fire-screen in
my sitting-room here, which has been
disturbing me quite seriously all this winter.
It represents a group of Boers—when the
tapestry was made I take it the word was
spelt *boors*—of various ages and sexes, but
all equally convulsed with laughter. The
central figure is a big, square-jawed, good-
natured looking fellow, who holds aloft in his
hands a tiny, red-coated toy manikin, which he
is causing to perform ridiculous antics for the
amusement of a solid infant of two or three
years old, who is trying to reach it. At a
table close by an old man sits eating, in a
suit of what appears to be greasy grey corduroys.
He also grins with satisfaction at the perform-
ance. So does a woman — presumably the
mother of the solid infant — who looks back
laughingly from a doorway, over the dish which
she carries in her hands. Other Boers, or boors,
are to be seen in the background, all equally

I

convulsed by the ludicrous figure cut by little
Red-coat; all distorting jaws—wide enough by
nature—into grimaces expressive of appreciation
at his ridiculous position.

Since the original of this piece of tapestry
was painted over three hundred years ago by
a painter named Teniers, it is not at all likely
that it was meant to represent our Boers of
to-day, nor that the ridiculous little manikin in
the red coat could be meant for an unfortunate
Rooinek! In spite of that fact I have been
unable for months to endure to look at this side
of my harmless little fire-screen. Every morning
on entering my sitting-room my first act has
been to push it up through its sliding groove,
until only a pair of prodigiously stout calves,
and one infant's shoe remain to be seen. To-
day—and I write the fact down as a sign of
changed times — my fire - screen remains un-
touched! More than this, I have found a
malignant satisfaction in sitting down before it,
and, as I warmed my feet—damp with gardening operations—surveying the row of grinning
faces, with the little red manikin still performing
his degrading antics in their midst.

"Laugh away, my friends!" I remarked.
"Laugh away! Make the most of your time.
Don't disturb yourselves pray on my account.
The unfortunate *Rooinek* is no doubt, as you
say, a very ridiculous and helpless sort of

creature. At the same time don't be too sure that he may not make a sudden leap yet out of your fingers! Stranger things have happened."

So many caricaturists, friendly and unfriendly, have made capital out of this struggle of ours that I rather wonder none of them seem to have hit upon this familiar Teniers. That accuracy that pertains to all genius is plainly visible, moreover, as one looks at it, for the portraits—evidently they are portraits—might be those of any group of our worthy enemies to-day. As for the old fellow at the table, it might be Oom Paul himself in proper person ; the same air of somewhat sanctimonious rectitude ; the same broad fleshy nose, the same protruding chin, the same semicircular sweep of grizzled beard. It sets one reflecting upon the persistency of national types. Centuries rise, and grow, and fade away; wars are made and cease again, but probably few things in this fluctuating world change so little, or with such a snail-like slowness, as the few broad lines upon which the characteristics of any given race have once got themselves legibly inscribed.

MARCH 1, 1900

SURELY we need no satirist to point out the ironies of life, for they are for ever with us! Here is the latest in my own experience :—

After all my arrangements, my care about telegrams, my determination not to be defrauded of even half an hour's satisfaction, I have heard at last of the relief of Ladysmith from a child by the roadside; from a child? nay but from a baby, a smudgy-faced cottage infant, that could barely walk, and certainly was quite unable to talk! It happened in this wise. I was hurrying along the lane on my way to take the train for Godalming, having waited till the last minute in hopes of a telegram which never came. My morning papers had told me nothing, or nothing beyond vague surmises, which I was quite competent to provide for myself; consequently I was famishing for more substantial fare. I had nearly reached the village, and was hurrying round the last corner. Suddenly out of one of the cottage doors came this creature, dragging after it a stick with something red tied to it, which I entirely failed to distinguish as having been even intended for a flag. Either it stumbled, or from sheer force of circumstances simply sat down in the middle of the road, right in front of me. I was delayed an instant, and in that instant out flew its mother, and plucked it to its feet again, with a sound maternal smack.

"There ain't no sense in yer being run over, is there, ye little fule, not if Ladysmith *is* relieved!"

"Ladysmith!" I was upon the two of them in an instant, and had seized the bigger one by the arm, though she was not an acquaintance of mine.

"What did you say? *Is* Ladysmith relieved?"

"Lor bless you ma'am, don't you know? Why hours and hours ago! *We* heard of it a little afore eleven we did!"

"But are you certain? Is there no mistake this time?"

"Mistake? Bless you, no ma'am, there ain't no mistake! Why it were stuck up at the office by Mr. Smith hisself, just gone quarter to the hour. I was a-coming along with my husband's second breakfast, for he's working now for Mr. Bellew at the Mills. So as I was passing close to the office 'Whatever is all this about,' thinks I, for there was eight or ten people a-standin' there, and a-readin' somethink. And with that I sees——"

I too had seen something! A flag—unmistakably a Union Jack — hanging near the Church, I had overlooked it in my hurry. At sight of that, excitement, combined with the fear of missing my train, overcame my politeness, and I flew down the lane in the direction of the station.

The train was caught, but only by the narrowest margin. I sprang into a carriage, all but shaking hands as I did so with an absolutely unknown old gentleman, who was its only other occupant. Everyone knows the shrinking, the more than maidenly dread of the solitary travelling *he*, for the unknown travelling *she*, however harmless the latter may look. On this occasion public interest overcame even that terror. As a river bursts through its banks, so my old gentleman burst into a torrent of repressed information. He had just come from London; he had witnessed the scene at the Mansion House; he described to me the Lord Mayor coming to the window with a telegram in his hands; he dilated upon the crowds, the cheering, the flags, the block in the streets; above all upon the central fact of the situation, which was that he had himself been thereby made twenty minutes late at his board, or meeting, whatever it was. " For the first time in twenty-five years!—the very first time! They couldn't make out *what* had happened to me; thought I must have been run over!" he assured me several times between Guildford and Godalming.

Well, well, it has come at last! All is right, all is well, and we may go back to our own little concerns; our housekeepings, and our marketings, our weedings, and our seed-sowing, with lighter; let us hope, perhaps also, with a trifle gratefuller hearts?

MARCH 3, 1900

OUR good old Cuttle is leaving us; will be gone by this time next week, and I feel more sorry than seems quite reasonable! To-day, when we began talking the matter over together, a suspicious huskiness in my voice warned me that I should do well to get away from the subject before my character for propriety was quite lost!

It is better I know for many reasons that he should leave. He cannot, indeed will not, undertake sole charge of both flower and kitchen garden, and to have anyone over him in either department is not to be dreamed of. Moreover his own home is four miles away, all up and down a long crooked lane, and a walk like that after a hard day's work would be enough to try anyone half his age. Under ordinary circumstances the departure of a man who, though he has been with us now nearly three years, came at first as a mere jobber, would be a small affair on either side. Our poor old Cuttle is however so identified with the very existence of this little possession of ours that to lose him seems like losing a piece, and moreover a considerable piece of it. If the pegs and the marking-tapes have been our contributions, all the solid work, the earth turning and delving, the trenching, the grass - sowing, the cutting down of trees, above all the interminable pitchfork operations, have been his, and his satellite's. Surely then he has a right to regard himself as its creator? Our good, old, kindly, argumentative Cuttle! The familiar little nooks and corners, cultivated, wild, half wild, will hardly seem so entirely themselves ; hardly so intimately familiar, without your friendly face !

MARCH 5, 1900

ALLAH be praised for a leisurely life! I have
been visiting A. R. D., whose days are filled
with large and various activities; whose responsi-
bilities are great; whose hours of work are long;
of leisure few and scanty.   I admire such indomitable workers, with an admiration which increases
with every year I live, but I envy them, Oh ye
gods, not at all!

"Cling to the peace of obscurity; they shall
be happy that love thee."   Where, I wonder,
have I acquired that rather ignominious injunc-
tion?   There is a seventeenth-century flavour
about it which makes it sound respectable, yet
at bottom I suppose it is merely a counsel of
laziness.   Work, far from the curse, is the alleviation of the curse; of that I am as convinced as
anybody.   At the same time a good deal of the
work that goes on around one seems to be rather
the product of the unasked volition of the worker,
than of any violent external necessity.   Obscurity
and laziness moreover are far from interchange-

able terms, seeing that the majority of the hard-
workers of the world are, and as a necessity
always will be, obscure.   It is only in our little
fussy artistic or literary coteries that the two ideas
have attained to a sort of accidental connection.
Personally I have a relish, I might almost say
a passion for obscurity.   The retort is of course
easy, and I am able to reply to myself that
the alternative has never been pressed upon my
attention with any very urgent insistence.   That
is true, but does not really affect the matter.
Honestly, I do regard obscurity as a blessing,
apart from such satisfactions it may provide for
laziness.   For what does it mean?   It means
that you belong to yourself; that you have your
years, your days, hours, and minutes undisposed
of, unbargained for, unwatched, and unwished
for by anybody.   It means that you are free
to go in and out without witnesses; free as
the grass, free rather as the birds of the air.
Further, I am inclined to think that only
Obscurity can properly and heartily enjoy his
sunsets, moon-rises, spring mornings, running
streams, first flowers, and all the rest of the good
cheap joys that lie about his path.   The known
and admired person is expected to make capital
out of such matters, and he probably does so too,
poor fellow!   Yet upon the untrammelled enjoyment of such things how much, not only of the
satisfaction, but of the peace of life depends?

As was said by one—who, by the way, was very far himself from being an Obscurity—" Nothing startles me beyond the moment. A setting sun will always set me to rights, and if a sparrow comes hopping to my window, I can take part in its existence, and pick about the gravel."

A SENTIMENTALIST sleeps in nearly
everyone, whether he is aware of the fact
or not; just as we are all potential poets or
lovers, though some of us undoubtedly under
rather a deep disguise. My particular vein of
sentiment has lately taken the form of linking
together sundry small spots here with others
far away, upon the other side of St. George's
boisterous channel. Thus I have a Burren
corner, a West Galway corner, a Kerry corner,
a Kildare corner, even a green memento or two
of the great lost forest of Ossory, of which only
a few shadowy remnants survive to a remote, but
happily not an indifferent generation.

That pleasure is to be found in such childish-
ness might at first sight seem incredible. Since
it is so, there is no use, however, in refusing to
recognise it oneself. Take the Burren, for
instance. Burren the wild, the remote, the
austere, the solitary; to the few who know it
a region absolutely unique, with its cyclopean

terraces sloping slowly to the waves, that moan
and mutter eternally around their bases. To
represent the Burren—even the Burren plants
—by three or four tiers of stones, which are not
even limestones, might well seem even to oneself
the very acme of absurdity. I refuse however
to be ashamed of it, and if my Dryas octopetala
and my Helianthemum canum, my Potentilla
fruticosa, and my Cystopteris fragilis would but
accept such hospitality as I can offer them;
would but pretend that fragments of lime rubbish
are slabs of limestone, I should be content, and
ask no more of them.

Some are kindly enough, but others are hope-
lessly supercilious, and I am at my wits' end
how to cater for them. If distinguished visitors would only condescend to mention their
wants plainly, how gladly, I have often thought,
would one hasten to satisfy them. When they
merely look disgusted, and, after sulking hope-
lessly for some months, die upon one's hands,
what is an unfortunate host or hostess to do?
Here is Helianthemum canum, for instance,
which for the last nine months I have been
keeping from dying, as it were by main force.
Up to now I have in a measure succeeded, and
have even occasionally flattered myself that it
was beginning to resign itself. I know perfectly
well however that it has in reality made up its
mind upon the subject, and that one of these

mornings I shall hurry out to my "Burren" corner, only to find Helianthemum canum looking black but satisfied, having just succeeded in dying triumphantly on my hands!

MARCH 8, 1900

THE pace at which some plants, no matter how discouraging the weather, manage to swell out their tissues, and to spring aloft under one's very eyes, is an unfailing marvel, and in this unpropitious soil the marvel seems all the greater. So many quite common plants decline to live in it in its natural state, that one's gratitude goes out all the more to the few that are willing to put up with us as we are. Foremost amongst such obliging vegetables stand the mulleins, and foremost amongst the mulleins stands that really noble person, Verbascum olympicum. If it has a fault it is that it is *too* good-natured, and *too* vigorous. Not only does it attain to its robust proportions at a rate that takes one's breath away, but further it increases so rapidly, and with such a reckless prodigality, as threatens to people the whole neighbourhood with its descendants. Seeing that each of such descendants requires as much space for its development as does its parent, the perplexed gardener wonders at times how he is to dispose of his too obliging property, and ends by being not a little embarrassed by his own wealth.

There was one day last summer, when, returning home after a short absence, and going into the garden, I was not a little startled to discover what a congregation of the giants we had unwittingly been entertaining. A giant may of course be highly ornamental, and a giant that is eight feet high, and of a bright canary-yellow throughout the greater part of that length, is almost bound to be so. There were —I took the trouble to count them—one hundred and eleven such giants at that moment all in flower together in the garden. Now considering that the proportions of that garden are not those of Kew or Versailles, there is no denying that one hundred and eleven bright yellow giants, all occupying it at the same time, affected the mind with a certain sense of surplusage! They stood in rows along the grassy paths; they shouldered one another, and everything else out of any place they had been allowed to spring up in; they appeared unexpectedly in out-of-the-way corners of the copse, where the elderly oak-scrub found itself reduced to the position of a mere underling at the feet of these aspiring biennials. To come suddenly round a corner

K

was to receive an impression of being surrounded
by a crowd of gigantic, lemon-coated attend-
ants, all standing respectfully at attention, an experience naturally rather trying to mere modest
humanity.

There is another equally large and complacent
biennial, which, on account perhaps of that
very complacence, I find myself constantly
treating with the scantiest civility. It has not
I think quite the solid strength and impressive
bearing of the great mullein, but as regards
height, is often even more gigantesque. This is
the large variety of Œnothera biennis, familiar
to most people as Œnothera Lamarckiana, but
possessing no English name that I am aware of
beyond the generic, and not very descriptive
one of " Evening primrose." There are a good
many varieties of evening primroses in gardens,
both perennials and biennials, and a few true
species, of which missouriensis, otherwise macro-
carpa, is undoubtedly one of the best. Lamarckiana on the other hand is hardly a subject for the
garden proper. As a tenant of steep banks, of
rough borders ; of all sorts of half, or three-
quarter wild places, it has in this soil no com-
petitor, or only finds such competitors in the two
biggest of the mulleins.

I have been trying this year the experiment
of planting it along both sides of the green

walk that crosses the upper part of our copse.
Whether it will endure the amount of shade
that it will find there remains to be seen.
It is a sun-lover by nature, like most of its
tribe, but its growth is so redundant that
a little curtailment of it will do it no great
harm. Though less spreading, it requires almost
more room than the verbascums, for, if the
space it covers is less, it is a true biennial,
never failing in my experience to flower the
year after it is sown. With Verbascum olympicum this is not so. There are some here
at this moment that were sown three years
ago, and have not yet flowered. They will
do so no doubt this year, and with that event
the cycle of their existence ends. The worst
is that the gap they leave when they die is
large ; moreover, as in the case of foxgloves,
the black stump is both an ugly object in
itself, and a difficult one to get rid of. When
are we to possess a really good perennial
foxglove I wonder ? There is a perennial
yellow one, but it is a poor thing, hardly
worthy of its name. Perennial verbascums are
also few in number, most of the family showing
a more or less aloe-like fashion of flowering.
In their case one is able to console oneself.
The imagination grows a trifle giddy in fact
at the thought of every mullein one has seen

spring from seed remaining as a permanent possession ; always equally towering, and equally clamorous of space and sunlight.   Many-acred would be the garden that could support them all !

MARCH 19, 1900

SOME way back in this diary I was unwise enough to inveigh against that "pleasant herb called Vanity," especially in its relation to gardens. A greater error I now feel there could not be, and I am convinced that if we only took care to cultivate a sufficient supply of it, it would not only be a satisfaction in itself, but an immense stimulus to the successful cultivation of all other desirable plants.

This is not, I am aware, the general view. The general idea being that the herb in question is a mere weed, one that will not only grow everywhere, and at all seasons, but that grows the most luxuriantly upon the poorest soil. Now this is certainly not the case. What amount of it is grown in other gardens I cannot say, no report —or only a very indirect one—being forwarded to any of the regular gardening periodicals. That there are poor varieties of it I am willing to admit, but a really good "strain" is always worth securing, if it can be done legitimately, and so I am sure every successful gardener would be the first to say. So convinced do I feel of its value that there are many succulent, and quite wholesome vegetables, that I would gladly see thrown away in order to make room for more of it!

That admirable essayist, and, from his own account, horticulturist also, Sir Thomas Browne, evidently grew a good deal of it in *his* garden, though with the odd humour that prevails amongst its cultivators, he imagined that he had very little, in fact none at all. Here is the *Religio Medici*, so I have only to turn to his panegyric of it, a panegyric all the more satisfactory because he apparently intended it to be the reverse. Perhaps though, as Mr. Pepys would say, " That was in mirth."

" I thank God amongst those millions of vices I do inherit and hold from Adam, I have escaped this one." [Millions of vices! now may heaven help thee, Sir Thomas! however one must remember that he was a rhetorician.] " Those petty acquisitions, and reputed perfections, that advance and elevate the conceits of other men, add no feather unto mine. I have seen a grammarian tower and plume himself over a single line in Horace, and show more pride in the construction of one ode, than the Author in the composure of the whole book. For my own part, besides the jargon and patois of several provinces, I

understand no less than six languages; yet
I protest I have no higher conceit of myself
than had our fathers before the confusion of
Babel, when there was but one language in
the world, and none to boast himself either
linguist or critick. I have not only seen several
countries, beheld the nature of their climes, the
chorography of their provinces, topography of
their cities, but understand their several laws,
customs, and policies; yet cannot all this persuade the dullness of my spirit unto such an
opinion of myself as I behold in nimbler and
conceited heads, that never looked a degree
beyond their nests. I know the names, and
somewhat more, of all the constellations in my
horizon; yet I have seen a prating mariner, that
could only name the Pointers, and the North
star, out-talk me, and conceit himself a whole
sphere above me. I know most of the plants of
my country, and of those about me, yet . . ."

Nay Sir Thomas, dear Sir Thomas, let me
not follow thee longer in this vein, else might
one of the devoutest of thy followers lose some
share of that devoutness! I hastily ruffle thy
pages over, feeling certain before long of coming
upon thee in a worthier one.

.   .   .   .   .

I have been longer over my search than I
expected, having set my heart upon finding one

particular passage, which I failed to do, a fact hardly to be wondered at, since, as it turned out, there was no copy of *The Garden of Cyrus* in the house. I have found it however, at last, safely hidden, like a sprig of myrtle, in the tight embrace of an ancient notebook.

"But the quincunx of heaven runs low, and 'tis time to close the first parts of knowledge. We are unwilling to spin out our awaking thoughts into the phantasms of sleep, which often continueth precogitations, making cables, and cobwebs, and wildernesses of handsome graves. Beside Hippocrates hath spoke so little, and the oneirocritical (!) masters have left such frigid interpretations from plants, that there is little encouragement to dream of Paradise itself. Nor will the sweetest delights of gardens afford much comfort in sleep; wherein the dullness of that sense shakes hands with delectable odours; and, though in the bed of Cleopatra, can hardly with any delight raise up the ghost of a rose.

"Night, which Pagan theology could make the daughter of Chaos, affords no advantage to the description of order, although no lower than that mass can we derive its genealogy. All things began in order, so shall they end, and so shall they begin again; according to the Ordainer of order, and of the mystical mathematicks of the city of heaven.

" Though Somnus in Homer be sent to rouse
up Agamemnon, I find no such effects in these
drowsy approaches of sleep.   To keep our eyes
open longer were but to act our Antipodes.
The huntsmen are up in America, and they are
already past their first sleep in Persia.   But who
can be drowsy at that hour which freed us from
everlasting sleep ? or have slumbering thoughts
at that time when sleep itself must end, and, as
some conjecture, all shall awake again ? "

Most melodious of rhetoricians, and most
whimsical of prose-poets, I bid you a good-night.
For by a coincidence which you would be the
first to appreciate, twelve o'clock is striking even
as I copy your last line, and I light a bedroom
candle with the sound of those dim prognosti-
cations, and thunderous conjectures of yours still
ringing sonorously about my ears.   They do not
alarm me, however ; nay I would gladly carry
them with me past the ivory gate.   For, as you
yourself say—

" Happy are they that go to bed with grand
music like Pythagoras, or have ways to compose
the fantastical spirit, whose unruly wanderings
take off inward sleep, filling our heads with
St. Anthony's visions, or the dreams of Lipara,
in the sober chambers of rest."

MARCH 20, 1900

FROM the defence of Vanity, to the defence of England! "Attend to your transitions, my boy," is said to have been the reply of a veteran orator, when pressed by a junior for some axiom that would sum up the whole art of oratory in a sentence. Literature also, like oratory, has to attend to her transitions, else dire confusion, and the just indignation of her readers, is the result. The diarist stands upon a slightly different footing. If there is such a being as a literary libertine, or harmless law-breaker, he perhaps is entitled to the name. His pages are filled up according to no settled plan, and with an eye to no particular convention. He claims to be free as the wind upon the tree-tops, free as all our unwritten moods, which are rarely quite the same for many consecutive hours. Such at least, is the claim of this particular diarist. To-day, for instance, leaving the garden, and all that relates to it, to take care of themselves, he has wandered away upon the theme, of all things in the world, of *Invasion*, moved thereto, partly by the desire which assails us at all times, of dilating upon what one knows least, partly by the equally inborn desire of running counter to conventions upon which one has been brought up, and which have been instilled into one's mind ever since one could walk unaided.

That the difference between soldiers and civilians is an absolute difference, clear as glass, hard as adamant, is one of those conventions. Until the other day I never remember hearing it so much as questioned. Yet how does that fact now stand in the face of all that we have been hearing, seeing, reading about, during the last five months? If one thing more than another has been brought home to us by this present struggle it is that under modern conditions a civilian—without the slightest pretensions to be anything else, so long only as he is a good marksman—is not only as valuable, but under many circumstances, far *more* valuable than the average soldier, who as a rule can just shoot, and nothing more, who has all the finer parts of his art still to learn, and is not at all likely to learn it when he has no more leisurely target to practise upon than the living man.

It is upon the strength of this revolution that I have been indulging this morning in a private Invasion of my own, specially designed for the exaltation of the rifle-shooting civilian, in

whose doings I take a natural interest. Plans of
Invasion are always rather fascinating, whatever
the realities are likely to be. On this occasion
I have only allowed myself a very small and
cheap Invasion, just enough to put our rifle-
shooting civilian standing in it and asking how
he is to behave himself. It is not coming off in
the orthodox place, which I take to be nearly
opposite the bathing sands of Boulogne, but upon
quite a new theatre, namely upon the shores of
Dublin Bay. My invaders are probably French,
but may be anything else, it does not in the least
matter. Whoever they are they have succeeded
in evading the Channel Fleet, have run the gaunt-
let of the forts—no impossible feat—and have
disembarked some forty or fifty thousand strong
somewhere between the Bailey of Howth and the
foot of Bray Head.

As for their purpose in landing, so far as my
information extends, it is simply to do as much
damage as can be conveniently accomplished
within a given time. If the defending fleet remains entangled elsewhere, and they can be
reinforced, so much the better. In any case
France can afford to lose some twenty or thirty
thousand recruits in a good cause. Moreover
he would be a poor sort of Frenchman who for
the sake of burning, harassing, shooting, raiding,
racking, ruining, and generally running amuck,
amongst British possessions, would not run the

risk of capture, and the, not after all, very uncomfortable, entertainment of a prisoner of war.
Here, then, stands our military position ; and now
comes the question of what in such a case, are
the rights and duties of the ordinary, peaceable
but rifle-shooting civilian?

First let me clear the ground for myself
a little. In the course of certain profound re-
searches upon the whole art and practice of war
as laid down in the *Débâcle*, *La Guerre et la
Paix*, and other recondite manuals, I have learnt
that in the case of invasion the barrier between
civilians and professional soldiers is even stricter
and more menacing than at other times. The
soldier, let his capacity or incapacity be what it
may, is entitled in case of capture to honourable
treatment. He may be nearly starved to death,
if provisions run short, as the French soldier-
prisoners were after Sedan. He may be shot
out of hand, if he endeavours to escape, but with
these trifling exceptions he is a person having
definite rights and a definite status ; a person the
cold-blooded slaughter of whom would stamp the
perpetrator of such a deed as a brute, no gentleman, and a man generally to be avoided, even by
his own side. Turning now to the position of
a civilian during invasion, I learn, by studying
the same authorities, that he is an individual
without rights of any kind should he attempt—
no matter upon what provocation—to touch a

weapon in war time. Although the weapon in question be his own familiar rifle or fowling-piece; although the spot he proposes to defend with it is his own hearth, with his own wife and daughters standing beside it, he is liable—legally and honourably liable, for that is the whole point —to be led away from that hearth, settled comfortably with his back against the nearest wall, and then and there uncomplainingly shot, his wife and the rest of his family looking on. This I am assured, or used to be assured, is the whole law and the gospel, as the law and the gospel is laid down for military purposes; a law the carrying out of which is not only permitted, but is the bounden duty of every honourable soldier and Christian officer. In no other way, so I have always been told, could the protection of the civil population be guaranteed during invasion. If a man, merely because the property destroyed is his own, were free to pot—we call it nowadays to snipe—at the destroyer of that property, what in such a case would become, one was asked, of the poor defenceless soldiery?

So much for the old rule, now for its modern application. Bearing all this in mind, I look away to South Africa, and what do I see? I see a crowd of fighting men, upon hardly one of whom—our own regulars and militia of course excepted—can I succeed in discovering any of the recognisable marks of a soldier. Here and there one or two such may be discerned, but the bulk are purely and avowedly civilian. They have walked out of their shops, their farms, their offices, their counting - houses, their clubs, or wherever else they come from, precisely as we see them. They can shoot, or they think so; they can ride—more or less—but in spite of these accomplishments they are no more soldiers than is the diarist who dips this eminently civilian pen into this utterly unmilitary inkpot. If the German commanders of 1870 refused to see in the *francs tireurs* anything but unrecognisable freebooters; if Napoleon declined to accord the Tyrolese marksmen and their heroic leader decent treatment, mainly on the grounds that the latter was an innkeeper, what would either of them have said to the bulk of those fighting upon both sides to-day in South Africa?

All this, however, is merely preliminary. Our invasion is no problematic peril this time, but a peril that has actually arrived. They have *come*, the aggressors! they are already standing upon our sacred shore! the question now is what are we to do with them? Can there be any doubt upon that subject? Up, arm yourselves, and away! high and low, young and old, brave and the reverse—women first, as befits their daring! Up, and at the villains! Let them not carry their purpose an inch further. Let not one of them return to boast of where he has been!

Yet hark! what sound is that? Surely it is not the luncheon bell? How *exceedingly* inconvenient! Well, our invasion must be postponed for the moment. After all, as Peter Plymley wrote to his brother Abraham, "It is three centuries since an English pig has fallen in a fair battle upon English ground"; so, though this particular struggle is coming off not on English but Irish ground, it is not likely to be all over before this afternoon.

MARCH 20, 1900. 3 P.M.

THAT interruption disposed of, we now return to our Invasion. Owing, perhaps, to the dilatory nature of our proceedings, the invaders have already left the coast, and pushed their way some distance inland, the result being that matters are beginning to look exceedingly uncomfortable for the unfortunate invaded. The regular army in Ireland happens to be at an exceptionally low ebb. It has been heavily drawn on lately to fill up vacancies at the seat of war, no one in authority having of course dreamt of anything so improbable as a sudden incursion into Dublin Bay. The Commander-in-Chief is reported to be half dead with work and worry at the Royal Hospital. His subordinates are behaving like heroes. The " Polis "—otherwise the Royal Irish Constabulary —are doing soldiers' work, and doing it a good deal better than most soldiers. Dublin is believed to be for the moment safe, but the condition of the country immediately south of it is critical to a degree. No one seems to be certain what the

L

opinion of the bulk of the people really is. Invaders, especially French ones, are historically
dear to their hearts, but the thing has been
sprung upon them this time with rather uncomfortable rapidity, and there is something extremely
sickening, so everybody admits, about the smell
of burning roofs.

Immediately upon landing, the enemy established their headquarters, with no little strategical
discretion, in a naturally defensible position upon
the Wicklow Hills, from which point they are
cheerfully engaged in sending out raiding parties
over the whole of the adjacent country. The
portion of Kildare nearest Wicklow has already
been overrun, and most of its villages burnt,
despite their nearness to the Curragh ; Naas and
Sallins are reported as likely to be the next
assailed. The suddenness of the catastrophe has
strained the military resources almost to breaking
point, and the soldiers are forced to be kept
together, not only to defend the approaches to
the metropolis, but also in the hope of being able
to bring on a general engagement in some more
hopeful position than against the fortified camp
in Wicklow. The result is that, beyond a limited
number of constabulary, the general in command
of the district is unable to spare a man for the
protection of the smaller places.

Before that harassed and overdriven officer
there suddenly appears—the Civilian ! How

many, or how few, is a detail. Few or many
they are all civilians, undiluted, country-bred
civilians, good shots and good riders; men of
varying ages, but all with a more or less intimate
knowledge of the local conditions. They are—
but generalities are so unsatisfactory — let me
take one of them, and suppose myself to be
him, and I can be multiplied afterwards as
required. Here I am; big and strong, level-
headed and resolute; no boy—far from it—but
sound in health and vigorous, a local magnate
in a small way, fairly good at most sports, rather
more than fairly good at rifle-shooting; a familiar
figure formerly at Wimbledon, more recently at
Bisley. Nothing can be further from my inten-
tions than to obtrude my services; I wish that
clearly to be understood. At the same time if
I can be of any use under the circumstances,
you had better say so!

With South Africa fresh in all our minds, can
there be any question as to the answer? What
more desirable material could unfortunate, under-
manned commander have, or desire? As to
what he could do with me there are plenty of
answers ready. He might place me in certain
chosen positions, rifle and field-glass beside
me, and desire me to pick off certain of the
enemy's officers, who are known to be surveying
the country. He might fill a country house or
two with me and others like me, and so prepare

pleasant little surprises for those who expected
to find them vacant. He might do many
things, only—and this is the point I am trying
to arrive at—would he venture to do any of
them ? If such a man as I am representing
myself to be were liable to be treated as
the Germans in 1870 treated French fighting
civilians, including women, and as the French
would no doubt have treated German ones, in
such a case it is hard to see how any responsible
commander dare run such a risk, however great
his need, or our willingness to serve. Risks
are of course of the essence of war, but there
are risks and risks. No one proposes to hunt
with the hounds, and then run with the hares ;
to fight while fighting is reasonably safe, and
afterwards slip hurriedly back into mufti ; to
play a soldier's part, yet claim the immunities
of civilians. Let the risks be no worse than
those which any soldier runs, and our faithful
civilian is satisfied, and asks no more. There
are, however, risks which it is hardly proper,
hardly I may say decent, for any self-respecting
man to run. That our typical civilian would be
really liable in these days to be shot in cold
blood, most people would find a difficulty in
conceiving, yet how does he stand officially ?
above all, how does he stand internationally ?
Have the risks of so monstrous, so utterly
abhorrent a contingency, been once and for ever

removed? and if so, since when? This is the
point that one would like extremely to have
authoritatively cleared up, seeing that the number
of civilians, capable at a pinch of defending their
own homes, possibly even their own fields and
parishes, seem likely as the years go on to increase. Organised, or unorganised, the straight-
shooting civilian has arrived, and he proposes to
stay. He is still, however, an entirely new factor
in the body politic, and, like other new-comers,
he requires therefore to be neatly adjusted to the
rest. That under no circumstances he could be
of any use, few, I take it, would be bold enough
to assert. These are hardly days when any
possibly useful national asset can be left with
safety upon the shelf. Let our sturdy civilian
be able, in case of capture, to claim the same
amount of amenity that is accorded in all decent
warfare to the captured soldier, in that case
I should say—speaking, of course, merely as a
fool—that the more of him we had the better
and the more comfortable for all of us.

MARCH 26, 1900

A VIEW, a brand-new view, and in a garden
supposed to be viewless! That our best
point as regards scenery lies in the direction of
the Dorking downs, is I think beyond question.
The worst of it is that lying as they do nearly
due north of us, the more of them we show the
more the wind catches at our plants. Openings
upon this side have, consequently, to be thought
out with care, and executed only after long de-
liberation.

This time I think we are safe. A space of
copse, ending in a fence, over which in summer
tree-lupins and everlasting peas tumble together
in friendly confusion, has been cleared. What
was lately solid copse, fifteen to twenty feet high,
has sunk to a mere russet-coloured growth, just
bracken height, no more; three feet to four
feet, that is to say, rising occasionally to five.
This makes a broadish space, in which bracken
and bramble, stunted elder, seedling birch, two or
three low thorns, and some wild guelder-roses

sprout together. Past this, sweeping up from the region of the larches, comes our new grass walk, eleven feet wide, consequently a walk of pride to people who have hitherto subsisted upon two-foot tracks! With a fine easy curve it turns away to the south, making for the gate which divides the garden from the copse. That turn being shared by the new opening, will I think ensure that no new rush of cold air can come tearing in upon the flower-beds. But for this no hatchet or billhook would have been conducted to the spot by me. Our new little view is—*pace* our neighbour's opinions—a remarkably nice little view, but did it display Alps or Andes, in place of the despised Dorking downs, the right-minded gardener would in the latter case hesitate; might even feel in the end that it would be too dearly purchased.

Now for the next question, and a serious one. Are we to allow ourselves to make any garden use of this new clearing or not? This touches upon the larger question of meddling generally. To meddle, or not to meddle? Is it permissible —as regards what lies outside the strict garden boundaries—to interfere, or ought we to leave the whole matter to Nature, in other words to Chance?

To lay down the law dogmatically upon this point would be to lay it down for every garden in Great Britain, or all not girded by kitchen gardens, or ploughed fields. Such a prospect, though enticing, might take some little time to carry out. Confining oneself for the moment to the immediate case, one finds that like most other cases, political, or horticultural, it is mainly one of compromise. Were our copse beginning to dwindle perilously, then, with a politician of the last generation, I should exclaim "*Can't* you leave it alone?" Seeing that, though we have been chopping assiduously ever since we came, two-thirds of our space is still covered with un-invaded copse, the case seems to me to be a fair one for experiment.

That being decided upon, what to experiment with becomes the next question, and here aspect is clearly the ruling factor. That no early morning sun will reach the place even in summer is certain. Four respectable oaks, of quite a gentle-manly girth, stand along the fence, and forbid it. They are not near enough for their roots to do much damage, but the firstlings of the sun's rays they will certainly keep to themselves. This being so, there is a limit clearly as to what will answer. All things considered, especially with regard to the fact that the brambles could hardly be dis-lodged without a wrench which would disorganise everything, I am inclined to give my vote for more brambles, only this time civilised ones. There are plenty fortunately to choose from. There is, for instance, Rubus odoratus, showing a vigour, and a turn for colonisation hardly to be exceeded by the very wildest of wild brambles. There is the cut-leafed bramble; there is the bramble of the Nootka Sound; there is the white-washed bramble; there is the salmon-berry; the cloudberry; the bramble of the Rocky Mountains, and others, all of which I already in fancy see tossing themselves up and down the bracken, and over their wilder brethren, in one delicious froth of white or rose-coloured blossom.

Another, and a yet more fascinating vision, sweeping over the field of my mind, has for a moment given it pause. What of a jungle, not of brambles, but of roses? None of your trim standards, of course, but some of the freer kinds —Rosa alba, Rosa lucida, Rosa brunonis, with some Ayrshires, some Dundee ramblers, and one commanding thicket of the biggest of the Polyanthas? It is a heady vision, and as a portion of the natural "wildness" might intoxicate the brain of Lord Bacon himself. In gardening it does not do, however, to be too easily intoxicated. We have to keep a sober head; we have to look at the matter from all its points of view; there is the question of aspect, already touched upon; there is the question of soil; above all there is the question of fertilisation—dear, delicate word! No, we must not allow ourselves to be carried off our feet by any vision, however roseate. We have always

been a pair of sober horticulturists, and we will
continue to be so still.   Our rose-jungle must
wait.   It is only postponed : we will have it
yet, and in a better place.   Even if we never
did have it, even if the postponement had to be
an eternal one, is it not, one sometimes asks
oneself, the gardens that never have been planted
—"whose flowers ne'er fed the bee"; whose dusky
scented walks no foot has ever trod, that yield
the deepest, the most unqualified enjoyment ?
" Heard melodies are sweet, but those unheard
are sweeter."   What then of unseen gardens ?
What wealth of blossoms ! what a flood of sunshine, which yet never scorches ! what green and
translucent groves, which at the same time are
never damp ! what order, without the faintest
touch of formality ! what wildness, what heavenly
entanglements, without so much as an approach
to confusion !   But I perceive that I am again
wandering out of the domain of horticulture, into
a much less attainable region, and it may be as
well, therefore, to pause.

MARCH 28, 1900

H AD we embarked upon a little stone house, instead of a little red-brick one, should we, I wonder, have had the energy to bestow upon ourselves a small flagged and stone-walled garden as an adjunct to it? I doubt it. For one thing flagged gardens are, I imagine, costly affairs. Moreover I have never myself seen a new one that appealed to me as quite satisfactory. An old, grey-walled, and grey-flagged garden, as part of an old, grey farmhouse, or manor, is one of the most ideal possessions that the heart of man could sigh after. Like most other ideal possessions, to have it, it is, unfortunately, necessary as a rule to have been born to it.

Be this as it may, I have never ceased to rejoice that we had the energy to embark at once upon our little red-brick garden. The comfort of knowing that there is always one spot sure to be clean, sure to be dry, sure to be a satisfaction to step into, even in such weather

as we have of late been afflicted with, is a boon
that can hardly be overrated. As a mere
matter of appearance, the red‑brick garden
seems to be at least as "natural" an appanage
of the red‑brick house as the little grey‑stone
garden of the grey‑stone one. Both require
a certain amount of thought and contrivance,
especially as regards proportion, but once this
is attained, they soon learn to wear that inevit‑
able aspect, which in garden making, as in all
the other arts, great and small, is the first,
and surely the least dispensable of all require‑
ments?

That the grey‑stone garden is on the whole
the higher species of the two I admit. At the
same time the red‑brick one has this great
advantage over its stony brother that it is
essentially a winter's day garden, whereas the
stone one may, and in bad weather does, look
grim, to the point of being almost forbidding.
In both gardens some amount of hindrance is apt
to arise with regard to the laying down of the
walks. Flagging is a costly process, and where
the walks are very narrow, the laying down
of stone flags must be a matter of some
difficulty. The same applies, though not quite
to the same extent, to the red‑brick garden.
That it ought to be tiled, just as the other
ought to be flagged, I feel sure. At the same
time good, red gravel, or even bricks, broken

fine, mixed with sand, and rolled, answers
fairly. Another question arises in the matter
of vases. Terra-cotta ones of the right design
are not easily come by in this country, and, when
come by, they often cost more than if imported
direct from Italy. These, however, are details,
while the question of what to plant in such
gardens is still more obviously an open one.
That the more of glaucous, grey-blue tints—such
as that found in the foliage of carnations—we
have the better, is I think certain, while if
small bushes are wanted, lavender will provide
the same shade. Where both walls and walks are
of red brick, blue, white and violet seem to be
the right prevailing colours; reds and yellows
only to be admitted slowly, and with precaution.
All this, however, savours of dogmatism!

The supreme moment for such little plots is
of course their spring-bulb time. Most people
call them Dutch gardens, and whether common
in Holland or not, the tulip undoubtedly seems
born to flourish in them. When the tulips are
over, plenty of other things come on however to
take their places. Pansies, for instance, never
look better than in such gardens, whether as a
carpet for tea-roses, or in beds by themselves.
The smaller campanulas, especially the white hair-
bells, the small double daisies, and a host of other
things of the same sort, answer perfectly, while,
if we want to stretch out our bulb season all

we can, sparaxis, ixias, bobartias, the early white gladioli, and others, are all ready to hand, followed by the various lesser irises, winding up, at perhaps their best point, with xiphium and xiphioides.

The one indispensable point—here again dogmatism appears!—is that such gardens should be so close to the house as to keep up the idea of being merely an adjunct, or flowery courtyard to it. With this idea in our minds anything like distance is fatal. You must be free to step into your garden from your door, or with no more interval than two or three steps, or the breadth of a gravel walk. Garden fanatics as many of us already are, and—as life increases in strenuousness—more and more will yearly become, it is our interest obviously to spin out our playtime all we can. Now nothing so helps us towards this, or so effectually counteracts our Arch-enemy, as to have some little settled place so cunningly contrived that even *his* malignity, backed by its worst agents—sleet, hail, fierce winds, cutting rains,—fails to reduce it to a condition of mere despairing sloppiness ; mere forlorn, and death-suggesting desolation.

MARCH 29, 1900

WHO would believe in being seriously tormented by a plague of oaks? Such nevertheless has been our lot for the last few weeks. As plagues go they are certainly better than locusts, not to speak of others that we read of in the Bible. For all that we find them quite troublesome enough. Although so young that they were only dropped from the parent bough last autumn, they already cling to the ground with all the tenacity of their ancestors; the most exasperated pull causing considerable fatigue to the puller, but producing no effect whatever upon the youthful athlete. Many of them are in the engaging condition of being still attached to their natal acorn, which, acting as a sort of grappling iron, effectually hinders their being drawn up, even through the soft soil of our flower-borders. Last year was a most bountiful one for acorns, and every sty in the neighbourhood revelled in plenty. Since we do not ourselves keep pigs, we hope that another season we may be less blessed!

Biologists have a theory—they would call it a law—which they call the law of "Multiplication in Geometrical Progression." By that law the plants of any region would, under favouring conditions, increase from a hundred to a thousandfold every year. Happily for people who wish to walk about they never really do anything of the sort; on the contrary, the population of any given district, apart from man's interference, remains for the most part all but stationary. Until a parent is considerate enough to die, and make way for it, every green child that is born is bound to die in its infancy. These little oaks of ours are an excellent example of that fact, as well as of the summary fashion with which Nature is in the habit of wielding her maternal sceptre. They are, as anyone can see, as hale and as vigorous as could be desired; hearts of oak, every one of them, and they know it. Not an oaklet amongst them but sees itself in nightly visions as an umbrageous giant, lifting high in air a mighty trunk, and spreading out branches that all the fowls of the air could lodge upon with comfort. Alas, for so much prospective dignity! Every one of these youthful monarchs is doomed to an early death, and it is merely a question of what stage of immaturity he will be called upon to perish at!

There is yet another biological dictum which these deluded young sovereigns may serve to illustrate. Before Darwin, or any other expositor, laid it down in prose, it had been already laid down in unforgettable verse—thus :—

> "No being on this earthly ball
> Is like another, all and all."

Nothing certainly on this earthly ball can be truer. Never two living beings came into the world precisely alike, and these baby oaks differ each of them in some imperceptible fashion from its baby brother. Here is a handful plucked at random out of the flower-beds that will prove it. In this one that I hold in my fingers, it is easy to see that the future giant would have been a somewhat thick-set, and stunted colossus. This one again has already a tendency to self-division, and would probably have ended by becoming forked. Yet again this one would, if it had been spared—appropriate phrase—have grown up to be the very ideal of oaks ; a glory of the woods ; star-proof ; sun-proof ; magnificent in its life, and in its death destined to be converted into the very straightest and most wind-defying of masts. This last, by the way, is not a loss that we need delay to weep over, seeing that long before it could have reached maturity, masts will in all probability have gone to join the other relics of the past ; even yachts

M

being converted probably by that time into little electrical monsters, with ingenious arrangements for enabling them to become submarine ones, whenever the wars of that date threaten to interfere with the comfort of their owners.

Poor baby oaks! They gave me a great deal of trouble to pull up, and now, with that inopportune remorse, sometimes ascribed to murderers, I am disposed to grow quite pitiful over them. They have been so spoilt, moreover, in the process, that they are not even worth putting into a flower-vase. Imagine having been potentially capable of serving as the tutelary deity, the beloved shade, the *rendezvous* of all the lovers of a parish for possibly half a dozen generations, and being found actually unfit to fill a bow-pot for an hour! Could poet or pessimist hit upon instance of malicious destiny more dramatically or tragically complete?

A T last we are in April.   The winter corner is
turned, and a new era entered upon.   But
April this year is an incongruous sort of an April,
though the incongruity is possibly only in one's
own fancy.   We are apt to fashion our notions
of the becoming, and to expect Nature to con-
form to them.   A desperately dry April it certainly
is.   The days are hard, and cold, parched, and
nipping ; at night the wind howls, but with no
accompaniment of desirable drops.   The garden
cries to the sky for rain, but no rain falls upon it,
yet the only days I have spent in London were
days of unceasing downpour.   Such favouring of
the Metropolis at the expense of the country is
manifestly unjust.

April is such a lovely word, that it ought also
to be always a lovely thing.   If one imagines it
—or rather her—as she might appear to us in
dreams, or an allegory, we should deck her out
of course in the tenderest green.   Floating gossa-
mers would hover around her ; small pink buds

would bend down to kiss her small pink feet. So encompassed she would come to meet us along the wood paths, a vision of grace and maidenly beauty ; the traditional smile on her lips, the equally traditional tear in her eye. She would look up in our faces with an appealing glance, and then begin suddenly to weep, she herself knew not why. A maiden with the most maidenly of dreams, enclosing a whole enchanted world of visionary hopes, fears, delights, anticipations, which it would be the dull business of Experience to dissipate as the year rolled on.

But April, as she presents herself before us this year, is not that sort of maiden at all. She is a remarkably uncompromising sort of young woman, with hardly any visible green about her costume. She does not care for the colour apparently, but prefers drabs, and greys, and browns. As for tears she is not nearly as much given to them as we could desire. She thinks poorly of them evidently, and considers them out of date. Her smiles too are doled out in the same penurious fashion as her tears. She gives us what no doubt she considers our due of both, but nothing to spare. Her impulses are all dull, decorous, mechanical ; as for her feet, far from being bare, they are clad in warm winter shoes and stockings, which indeed they have every reason to be.

Doubtless I am old-fashioned, but I cannot

admire such sedate damsels. Give me a little
more spontaneity ; a little more youthful impetu-
osity and dash—

> "Robes loosely flowing, hair as free ;
> Such sweet neglect more taketh me."

To drop metaphor, which has a tendency
to drop itself, we are in despair over this
dryness, and as a consequence have had to
resort already to the aid of our watering-pots.
Now in April the watering - pot ought in my
opinion to be still reposing in its tool shed, with
the early spider weaving his first web across its
spout. So strongly is this impressed upon my
mind that I feel as if there were something illicit,
something I might almost go so far as to call
unprincipled, in resorting to its assistance thus
prematurely. After all though, a gardener's first
virtue, I reflect, is to save his plants, and unless
we promptly take some step of the kind, ours for
a surety will for the most part die.

APRIL 11, 1900

ONE advantage we have secured out of our dry April. Ever since our arrival we have wanted an additional water-stand for the garden, but various causes, chiefly I think dislike to making any more inroads upon the bracken, have hindered us from setting one up. When it comes to dragging watering-pots several hundred yards while the year is still only three months old, imagination pictures what fatigues will be ours in July and August. A new stand accordingly has been established, and an ugly scar the laying of it has made through the copse. Now however that part of the business is done; the grass sods, carefully laid on one side, are back in their places again, and one must only hope that the bracken, safely curled away underground, knows little or nothing about the transaction.

As its practical outcome we have, rising out of the ground, a short stiff pipe of lead, which has been more or less dexterously hidden away

in the heart of one of our stunted oaks. I am
ashamed to confess the intense, the childish
satisfaction I found this morning in turning our
new tap for the first time, and seeing the water
gush out in one free bound, as if glad of its
escape ; looking as clear too, as if newly come
from the heart of a glacier, or upon its way
to the edge of some Atlantic cliff, there to be
caught by the wind, as I have often seen it
caught, and sent back high overhead, in one
dancing, rainbow-coloured feather of light.

" Take you at your commonest, at your ugliest,
and what a lovely thing you are ! " I thought,
as I let the tap run for a few minutes, and stood
to watch the water beginning to create little rills
and runnels for itself, and to feed the dry copse,
the dead leaves, brambles, withered bracken,
everything within reach, with the first full rush
of its benevolence.

I do not know that I am more given than other
people to proclaiming aloud that I have too many
blessings ; that Nature has been too generous, and
too bountiful in her benefits on my behalf. Now
and then however it has occurred to me to ask
myself what I—or, for that matter, other people
—have done to deserve this free unstinted gift of
clear, pure water. In and out of our houses ;
through our pipes and conduits ; into all our
tubs and washhand basins, it flows and flows
continually, and we take it as an absolute matter

of course that it should do so, rarely even taking the trouble to say " Thank you."

By way of commentary upon the above reflection I have just taken up a newspaper from the table, and this is what has met my eye.   It is an extract apparently out of a letter home.

" We found some water at last near Stinkfontein "—suggestive name—" but the place was very shallow, and the mud black and deep.   We could not get the horses to look at it, but the men drank it greedily, and drank it too at the only place where they could reach it, which was where the hoofs had churned it into a blackish liquor, thick as soup."

Poor Tommy!   Yet there are people who declare that you are not fond of water!   Evidently this is another of those libels of which you have been too long the subject.

APRIL 17, 1900

THE west wind this morning had a rolling sonorousness which sent my thoughts flying, swift as light, across all the little intervening ridges, over the plains, over the villages, across endless housetops, through multitudinous suburbs, over the big, ugly, stately town ; out again, over fresh sweeps of more or less encumbered green fields, hedgerows, lanes, roads ; past meadows and orchards, redolent of centuries of care ; past brickfields and coalfields, redolent only of defiling greed ; over a fretful space of sea ; across more fields, less enclosed, less cultivated, but certainly not less green. On and on breathlessly, until I stood—free of all encumbrances, free of any thought of luggage, conveyance, or the need of a roof to shelter under—upon a very familiar spot, close to the tumbling breast of the Atlantic.

The clearness, or lack of clearness, with which certain familiar spots rise before the eye is one of the minor mysteries of life ; mysteries which like many larger ones we are never likely to clear up entirely to our satisfaction. There are moments in my experience when such a spot as this that I am thinking of, is in a sense *more* vivid to me away from it than if I were standing there in person; when every tuft of bog myrtle becomes clearly visible; every yard of "drift" or of "boulder clay" shows in its entirety; the very stones fallen from them, and lying like small cannon-balls upon the beach, being all able to be counted. The waves toss; the clouds roll wearily; the seaweed rises and falls, as it naturally would. No scene in a cinematograph could by any possibility be clearer.

This is the vivid condition. An hour later one tries to conjure up the same familiar scene, and not a detail will rise to one's bidding. Not a leaf, not a stone, not a wave will become manifest. Clearness is gone. A dull, blurred impression is all that remains. The landscape as a whole may be there, but its details are lost. That living, multitudinous - tinted foreground has vanished as though it had never existed.

It must have been the scent of the bog plants which conferred that momentary impression upon me this morning. That scents "open the wards of memory with a key" we all know. They do more, for they sweep away for the moment those films which ordinarily cover the

mental eye, so that during that moment we really
do see.   Of all scents commend me for this
awakening quality to the boggy ones.   They
alone in my experience are really transformatory.
For the brief time that their aroma is in one's
nostrils one actually *is* in the place that they
recall.

It is a proof of the demoralising effect of
ownership that one of my first impulses nowadays is a desire to transfer the plants that I see,
sometimes that I merely remember, from where
they are to where I happen to want them.   Yet,
when one thinks of it, what an outrage!   Why
should one desire to do anything of the sort?
Conceive the contrast, the downfall; the roomi-
ness, the elemental breadth, the cool, rain-satu-
rated comfort of the one setting; the cramped
limitation, the unpalatable dryness of the other.
Not that I would for worlds disparage our own
faithful coppice; to do so would be to show myself the merest of ingrates.   Was I not an alien,
and did it not befriend me?   Was I not roofless,
and did it not offer its soil for us to lift a roof
over?   Still, when one tries to place the one
scene beside the other the contrast becomes
farcical.   The very wind—the cold, unsentimental
wind—must be sensible of such a difference.
How much more then a root-extending, acutely
sensitive, living thing!

I have a profound affection for bog plants,

which I hope some of them respond to, for they thrive fairly. Others are exceedingly difficult to establish, and rarely look anything but starved and homesick. Amongst these are the butterworts. Why the translation should so particularly affect them I have yet to learn, but the fact is unmistakable. Not all the water of all our taps, not all the peat of all our hillsides will persuade them to be contented. In vain I have wooed them with the wettest spots I could find; in vain erected poor semblances of tussocks for their benefit; have puddled the peat till it seemed impossible that any creature unprovided with eyes could distinguish it from a bit of real bog. No, die they will, and die they hitherto always have.

The sundews, on the other hand, are much less hard to please. Indeed, considering that at least one species grows wild within a few miles of us, it would be the height of affectation were they to refuse to tolerate us. I find myself falling into the habit of thinking that I am inhabiting here a region of eternal thirstiness, devoid of the materials of sustaining any vegetable more requiring in the matter of water than a gaillardia. Yet, when one considers the matter seriously, England is not precisely the Great Sahara! There are brown streams, purling brooks, dripping wells, rushy meadows, even puddles and bog-holes, to be found a good deal nearer to this spot than the Atlantic. We are purblind citizens all of us; apt to dogmatise largely upon an uncommonly small substratum of knowledge. Like the moles and the blindworms we know remarkably well the few inches that we can actually feel and touch; but with regard to what John Locke calls "the rest of the vast expansum," that we give up to fog and practical non-existence, thereby saving ourselves from the trouble of knowing anything about it.

APRIL 18, 1900

YET even dull, and quite unfeathered bipeds have their glimmerings now and then of sense, and of instinct.   There are hours in which the great Mother befriends them, as she does the rest of her two-legged, four-legged, or many-legged offspring.   That she should continue to do so is I think amiable, and rather surprising on her part, when one considers how they disobey and deride her ; how they sit day after day in stuffy rooms, eating dinners of many courses ; hardly ever getting up to see the sun rise, or doing any of the other things she directs, and which her better-behaved scholars invariably do.

In spite of this, when the right winds blow, when the spring is afoot, and the leaves are beginning to bud, she allows the old visions to return to them.   She brings back the old voices from the old haunts, to whisper once more in their ears, so that for the moment they forget the years that the locust has eaten, and their own incredible stupidities, and all that has been, and time rolls itself up like a scroll, and they are once again in very deed, though but for a little while, as they once were.

There is a spot in a hill-wood barely a mile from this door, to which I have been a good many times this spring, and which each time I go gives me a curiously homely feeling. Ireland seems to breathe in it, even West Ireland, though I can hardly say why, the only apparent reason being the rather unpatriotic one that the fir trees, of which the wood consists, have been sadly neglected. It covers an unusually steep bit of hillside, and below expands into a tangle of brakes and brambles, circling about a hollow place, which in my mind's eye I conceive to be a boggy pool, though, were I to clamber down to it, I should probably find it to be dust-dry. Far and near not a roof is within sight, else were that illusion for a certainty lost. Moreover, the only bit of distance visible seems to be houseless also, and in these grey, rather despondent-looking spring days wears just a touch of that wistful indefiniteness, the lack of which, one is apt to assert, amongst many beauties, to be England's most conspicuous blemish.

Until the last great summons comes for us, we can never, happily, entirely lose what has once formed a part of our little mental patrimony. We may deliberately discard it, or, what oftener happens, it may get unintentionally overlaid with other matters, so that it appears to be gone, but a little search, or some happy accident, brings it flying swiftly back, and the pleasure of that repossession is so great that it seems almost worth while that the thing should have been temporarily mislaid.

Of all such inalienable possessions the love of out-of-door life is surely the most inalienable? And is it not profoundly natural that it should be so? For this race, to which one belongs, was after all born under an open sky, even though every individual of which it is composed may have been born to-day under roofs. We do not any longer require the comfort of sheltering boughs, nor yet to nestle at night in moss-lined hollows, but the thought of such places still lurks in our blood, and the life of out-of-doors remains as much a part of the natural inheritance of a man, as it is a part of the inheritance of a fox, or of a wood-pigeon, or of a tiger moth.

Back, back—like the touch of half-forgotten greetings—comes a flood of remembrances to the heart. Back flows the old stream along its old channels. No longer tearing along with a wild tumultuous rush, but still sweeping by, full and clear, with a pleasant afternoon patter, and showing many an unlooked - for nook, many a forgotten corner along its banks, once we surrender ourselves frankly to its guidance. Back the scenes return ; ever back and back ;

now vividly; now with a dream-like vagueness;
scenes, some of them, that we have ourselves
known, others to which we have only as it were
a communal right. Waking hours under the
flickering shade of leaves; life as it was lived in
a larger, freer world; a world without walls or
hedgerows; without sign-posts, or notice-boards;
a world without towns, or smoke; without dust,
or crowds.

It has been often debated, and not perhaps
very profitably, which of two types of men see
deepest into that great arcanum of life which we
roughly call Nature. Is it the Man of Science,
whose business it is to chronicle what he sees
and learns, but who must never travel half an
inch beyond his brief? who must cling to fact, as
the samphire-picker clings to his rope, and never
for an instant relax his hold of it? Or is it on
the other hand the Singer, who is only too ready
to toss all fact to the winds, and to account it
mere dust, and dregs and dross, so he can
awaken in himself, and pass on to others, some
hint, some passing impression, of what he would
probably himself call the soul of things?

Time was when the barrier between these two
types was held to be an absolutely impassable
one. We call ours a prosaic age, but it is certainly one of its better points, and a mitigation
of that prose, that those barriers hardly appear
to us so absolutely impregnable as they once

N

were. If we have never seen a great scientist combined with a great poet it is at least not inconceivable that the world may some day behold such a combination. Even within the generation just over, and in utilitarian England, there have been one or two men who have given us at all events an inkling of so desirable a possibility.

Given a mind that can feed on knowledge, without becoming surfeited by it ; a mind to which it has become so familiar that it has grown to be as it were organic ; a mind for which facts are no longer heavy, but light, so that it can play with them, as an athlete plays with his iron balls, and send them flying aloft, like birds through the air. Given such a mind, so fed by knowledge, so constituted by nature, and it is not easy to see limits to the realms of thought and of discovery, to the feats of reconstruction, still more perhaps to the feats of reconciliation, which may not, some day or other, be open to it.

APRIL 26, 1900

THE reddening of our sundew patch has brought back to my mind various sundew experiments, carried on long since, with all the zeal of youth and enthusiasm. In this, as in every other walk of biology, the investigators of those days, amateur and scientist alike, followed with docility in the wake of their master. Darwin played the tune, and all the rest of us, great and small, danced to his piping.

To the best of my recollection my own investigations were chiefly carried on standing stork fashion upon a tussock, surrounded by an inky opacity, which threatened to draw the investigator downwards with a clutch, more tenacious and formidable than that of any sundew. To the faithful Irish botanist the poverty of the Flora of Ireland as compared with that of Great Britain has always been a serious humiliation. In this respect these Droseraceæ form an exception. Of the few British species all, I think, are to be found upon the bogs of the West of Ireland,

the largest of them—appropriately called anglica
—being much commoner in Ireland than elsewhere in these islands.

A very slight acquaintance with their habits
could hardly fail, I think, to convince even the
most sceptical that their roots are mainly em-
ployed as anchors, and water-pipes, while for
a supply of that nitrogen which every plant
requires they are chiefly, if not exclusively,
dependent upon insects. Of these the two lesser
species would appear to content themselves with
the smallest of Diptera and Lepidoptera, whereas
anglica will occasionally tackle larger prey, and I
have myself seen it with a good-sized moth (a
noctua) attached to and nearly covering the entire
disk, the long tentacle-like hairs being closely
inflected over the victim, whose struggles are
soon put an end to, once the sticky secretion
exuding from the hairs closes above the trachea.
When the leaf re-opens nearly the whole of the
insect (be it fly, moth or beetle) will be found to
have disappeared, even the wings being reduced
to a few glittering fragments. No animal substance in fact comes amiss ; fragments of bone,
hide, meat-fibrine, and even, according to one
authority, tooth enamel, softening, and in time
dissolving under the powerful solvent secreted
by the glands. Whether the Droseraceæ have
the power of attracting their prey, or must wait
until chance sends it within their clutches, seems

undecided. In the case of a little Portuguese relative, one Drosophylum lusitanicum (growing, unlike other members of the family, upon *dry* hills in the neighbourhood of Oporto) such a power appears undoubtedly to exist, the people of the neighbourhood using it as a flycatcher, and hanging it upon their walls for that express purpose.

This meat-eating habit or instinct (whichever we may agree to call it) is shared to a greater or less extent by all the Droseraceæ, such as the Venus's fly-trap, the Byblis gigantea of Australia, and a small but curious aquatic cousin, known to botanists by the formidable name of Aldrovanda vesiculosa, whose tiny leaves have the power of shutting vice-like over every unfortunate insect which approaches them, and which thus finds itself enclosed in a floating prison. If eminently characteristic of them, this carnivorousness is by no means confined however to the sundews, and their allies. If anything the Pinguiculas, for instance, rather exceed them in voracity. Few plants are at once so beautiful, and so interesting from the problems to which their distribution gives rise, as is the great Irish butterwort — Pinguicula grandiflora. Unknown to England and Scotland; unknown to the whole north of Europe; unknown even to the rest of Ireland; its viscid green rosettes may be seen on most of the lowlands of Kerry, and upon many of the

bogs of south Cork. For nine months of the
year that is all that there is to see. In June a
flower-stalk rises out of the centre of the rosette,
crowned with a pendulous bell of the most
pellucid, the most ethereal shade of violet. Happily for the susceptibilities of the investigator
this is not the flesh-eating portion of the plant,
that office being strictly confined to the leaves.
Stooping down and examining these leaves we
find that, whereas some are flat, others are
slightly dog-eared along the edges. If further
we unroll a few of the dog-ears we discover the
remains, not of one alone, but often of a dozen
unfortunate flies and midges, in all stages of
assimilation; some already half-digested, others
still alive, and struggling to escape from their
glutinous prison. If further we place a fragment
of bone, of meat, or indeed of any nitrogenous
substance, upon the edge of one of the fully
expanded leaves, we shall find that little by little
the leaf begins curling upwards, until the two
edges approach, and then join. Finally the
morsel is lost to sight, becoming entirely im-
mersed in its bath of secretion, where it remains
until all its nutritive parts are absorbed.

Viscous as the whole surface of the leaf is, it
does not seem as if this process of digestion was
carried on with the same rapidity in the centre
as at the sides, and, as there are in this case
no long hairs to act as locomotive organs, it

often happens that one may see flies and other
small insects lying partially dried up and useless
in the centre of the leaf. In one respect this
viscidity appears at first sight to be inconvenient,
the entire surface of the leaf being often covered
with twigs, leaves, particles of boggy fibre, and
such-like matters, which the plant has apparently
no power of getting rid of. In the end this may
prove however to be an advantage rather than
otherwise, since it has been ascertained that the
Pinguiculas feed, not alone on animal, but also
on vegetable substances; the extreme stickiness
of the leaves causes them moreover to act as a
chevaux - de - frise, thus hindering small but
industrious ants from making their way up the
flower-stalks to the corolla.

Yet another little group of bog - plants,
namely, the Utricularias, or bladderworts, are
meat eaters. In their case the fly-catching
apparatus is situated, not in the leaves, but in
certain small attached air - bladders, which are
constructed almost exactly upon the principle of
an eel-trap, and which, if opened, may generally
be found to contain flies. Thus we see how
discovery may be anticipated, and how one of
man's most boasted attributes — that of the
Destroyer — may be wrested from him by a
miserable little green bog-weed! Before the
first Celtic hunter flung spear at wolf or stag;
before the Firbolgs, or the Tuatha-da-Daanans

—cunning workers and craftsmen—had set up any gins or traps in the wilderness; before the first monk or abbot had arranged ingeniously devised weirs, wherein the salmon—seemingly by miracle—rang a bell to announce its own arrival; before any of these things had been done, or thought of, little Utricularia minor and little Utricularia intermedia had set up their own primitive green eel-traps in the yet un-visited wastes of Iar-Connaught.

MAY 5, 1900

FEW events are more gratifying than to find oneself taken more seriously by other people than by oneself, and I am pleased therefore to discover that our palpably artificial little pond has been taken possession of by a colony of frogs, which must have travelled some distance to make its acquaintance, frog-haunted ponds or even ditches being by no means abundant on these dry hillsides of ours.

I have never myself met more than one species of frog in these islands. Professor Bell, however, speaks of another, Rana Scotica, which he held to be distinct, but the difference seems to be mainly one of size. It is extremely difficult to persuade anyone who has noticed the multitudes of frogs which swarm in Ireland that they were only introduced there artificially, and as lately as the beginning of last century. Such, nevertheless, is the fact, and the date of the event is, moreover, a tolerably fixed one. It was a Dr. Gunthers, or Guithers, who, in the year 1705, turned out a handful of spawn into a ditch near Trinity College. For some years the frogs appear to have contented themselves with the neighbourhood of that University, but sixteen years later, in 1721, they were found forty miles away, from which point they seem to have rapidly extended themselves over the whole island. Incidentally the fact is confirmed by a great, if hardly a zoological authority, namely, Dean Swift. In his *Considerations about Maintaining the Poor*, which appeared in the year 1726, in the course of thundering against certain fire offices, which had the impertinence to be English, he declares that "their marks upon our houses spread faster and further than a colony of frogs." The portent, therefore, it is plain, had reached his ears.

Coincidences are attractive things, and it is satisfactory to discover that as regards earlier times we are again able to fortify our mere lay zoology upon the authority of an eminent ecclesiastic. This time it was St. Donatus, bishop of Etruria, who, writing in the ninth century, assured the world, upon his episcopal authority, that no frogs or toads existed, or, moreover, could exist in Ireland. Three centuries later Giraldus Cambrensis tells us, however, that in his time a frog was taken alive near Waterford, and brought into court, Robert de la Poer being then warden. "Whereat," he says, "Duvenold,

King of Ossory, a man of sense amongst his people, beat upon his head, and spake thus : 'That reptile is the bearer of doleful news to Ireland.'" Giraldus is careful, however, to assure us that "no man will venture to suppose that this reptile was ever born in Ireland, for the mud there does not, as in other countries, contain the germs from which frogs are bred"; indeed, in another part of the *Topographia Hibernica* we learn that frogs, toads, and snakes, if accidentally brought to Ireland, on being cast ashore, immediately "turning on their backs, do burst and die." This statement is corroborated by a still more illustrious authority, that of the Venerable Bede, whom Giraldus quotes as follows : " No reptile is found there" (in Ireland), "neither can any serpent live in it, for, though oft carried there out of Britain, so soon as the ship draws near the land, and *the scent of the air from off the shore reaches them*, immediately they die." So efficacious was the very dust of Ireland that on "gardens or other places in foreign lands being sprinkled with it, immediately all venomous reptiles are driven away." So, too, with fragments of the skins and bones of animals born and bred in Ireland ; indeed, parings from Irish manuscripts, and scraps of the leather with which Irish books were bound, were amongst the accredited cures for snakebite until well on in the Middle Ages. Of his own personal experience Giraldus relates to us how, upon a certain occasion, a thong of Irish leather was, in his presence, drawn round a toad, and that, "coming to the thong, the animal fell backward as if stunned. It then tried the opposite side of the circle, but, meeting the thong all round, it shrank from it as if it were pestiferous. At last, digging a hole with its feet in the centre of the circle, it disappeared in the presence of much people."

Our frogs and toads are not likely at present to become an affliction to us. Should they ever do so I must certainly send for some Irish leather, or, failing that, for a pinch of Irish dust, and try its effect upon them. An influence that has been vouched for by such a variety of authorities ought to retain something of its ancient potency. Scientific experiments in any case are always interesting!

MAY 8, 1900

RETURNING to our pond this morning to see whether the water-lilies propose flowering this season, I find that the frogs have been depositing spawn along its edges, so that the thongs of Irish leather may become necessary sooner than I expected!

All the same I am delighted to see the frog-spawn, for I have an affection for tadpoles. Youthful associations cluster pretty thickly around them, but apart from such a merely sentimental attachment, there is a satisfaction, I may say a zoologic thrill, about this transition of a water - living and water-breathing animal into an air-breathing one; a transition going on, moreover, not at some remote, and more or less dubious geologic age, but under one's very eyes, even, as in this case, in the middle of one's own decorous, shaven lawn.

It is difficult to remember that frogs breathe air as much as we do ourselves. Unlike ourselves, and their other zoologic betters, they do so, however, not by alternate contractions and

dilations of the chest, Nature not having provided
them with ribs, but by the doubtless more archaic
process of swallowing air. Not only would a frog
die if kept too long under water, but—seeing that
it can only swallow air by shutting its mouth—
were that mouth kept forcibly open it would equally
die, and from the same cause, namely, want of
breath. Tadpoles, on the other hand, are strictly
water-breathers, and until they have shed their
gills, have no more need to go to the surface to
breathe than a fish has. That, by the way is not
an absolutely accurate illustration, seeing that
certain fishes *do* need to go to the surface for
air. The famous Anabas, or "climbing perch"
of India, is such an air-breathing fish, the air
reaching it by means of cavities on either side
of its gills, and if prevented from reaching the
surface, and renewing the supply, it would "drown
like a dog," or so the scientists assert. Such
cases, however, can hardly be called normal.
Fishes that can live comfortably for days out of
the water, that can nest in a bush, and travel
across a particularly dry country, are not likely
to be met with in zoologic rambles about this
parish.

Returning to our Irish frogs, it is an odd fact,
especially considering their recent introduction,
that in addition to swarming over the lowlands,
and in every place dear to frogs, they have learnt
to climb long distances up hill, and to establish

themselves in ponds separated widely from any
others, often not even fed by streams, and
moreover destitute of nearly all other animal inhabitants, with the exception of certain minute
molluscs, which are believed by zoologists to
have reached them upon the feet of wading
birds, and that at such a remote period of time
that they have become what are practically new
species.

Many years ago, on reaching the top of
Mweelrea, the leading mountain of Connemara,
I remember my surprise at finding swarms of
young tadpoles wriggling along the margin of
a small pond, nearly upon the actual summit.
They were still in the engaging comma - like
stage, before legs had begun to dawn upon their
consciousness, and seemed to have remarkably
little to eat, for the water was crystal clear. The
pond was one of that attractive kind known as
corries, held by the geologists, doubtless truly,
to be of glacial origin ; a delicious clean-cut
oval ; pure rock, from marge to marge ; gouged,
as if by the chisel of Michael Angelo, from the
matrix in which it lay. But for the unmistakable
evidence of the tadpoles it would, to any reasonable imagination, have suggested the bath of
some mountain nymph very much sooner than
frog-spawn.

We are all of us to-day evolutionists, if some
of us still with a certain amount of reservation,

and to the evolutionist tadpoles must always prove interesting acquaintances. They provide us with at least an inkling as to the fashion in which your unadulterated water-breather may have been converted into an air-breather, and by means of no process more recondite than that of losing its gills. That such conversions do take place, and under certain circumstances remain permanent, has been proved in the well-known case of the axolotl, or Mexican gilled salamander. As long ago as the year 1867, while conducting some experiments at the Jardin des Plantes, M. Duméril startled the zoologic world of Paris by communicating the fact that, out of a number of axolotls kept in the collection there, about thirty had left the water, and had assumed the form of what had hitherto been regarded as an absolutely distinct genus of land salamander, known as amplystoma. This discovery made at the time a prodigious stir, not so much on account of a water-breathing creature losing its gills, and becoming an air-breather, for that was a phe-nomenon which might be seen every spring, and in most of the ditches round Paris, but because the axolotl was known to breed, and that it therefore appeared to indicate the exceedingly anomalous case of a larval form proving to be fertile.

How the feat of transformation was to be actually witnessed was the next problem, and it is pleasant to remember that it was through the energy and perseverance of a woman naturalist, Fraulein Marie von Chauvin, that the matter was finally cleared up. By continually damping the specimens of axolotl kept by her on land, and assiduously feeding them, she was able to preserve two out of five through the gradual process of decreasing their gill-tufts, and tail-fins, changing their skins, and so forth. Finally to her own and everyone's triumph, the complete amplystoma form was assumed, and the transformation was thereby accomplished. The world has seen a fair number of miracles since it began to run its course, and perhaps not the least difficult of those miracles to receive with absolute credulity have been some of its natural ones!

MAFEKING-DAY, 1900

IT is the nineteenth of May. S. S. has returned, and the east wind which has long been vexing our souls has departed for the moment, and a soft caressing zephyr blows seductively. The garden, comforted by recent showers, is smiling one broad smile from the red steps at the top of it to the new pergola at the bottom. And now this morning comes the news of the Relief of Mafeking. Joy for the victors ; joy for the nation ; joy for everything and everybody. Flags flutter from all the posts ; the dogs strut about in new tricolor rosettes ; "the air breaks into a mist with bells." All this is well, very well. Only ; only. A few lines coming by the same post, a single short note, and for one person that May sunshine is blotted out as effectually as though the very orb itself had perished. The garden with all its flowers ; the copse surrounding it, new clad in gala attire ; the whole cheerful little picture has become darkened ; its atmosphere changed ; its pleasant anticipations

turned into a simple mockery. Even to-day's
news sounds thin and unreal, and the tale of
Mafeking is as it were the tale of some defence
read of long since in an ancient, a seldom-
opened history, the actors and heroes of which
have long vanished and been forgotten. We
are but poor, bedimmed mirrors all of us, and
what we reflect is rarely the real thing, more
often only some blurred and distorted image
projected by our own sad selves.

MAY 26, 1900

THAT Nature is cruel is not to be denied; the evidences of that cruelty are written out large and red in every woodland, under every hedgerow. That she can be also unaccountably pitiful, or at all events take pains to appear so, is fortunately equally true, and it is a truth that at times comes very near to the heart. This morning at a very early hour there was a tenderness, a kind of hovering serenity over everything, that appealed to one like a benediction. The air itself seemed changed; sanctified. The familiar little paths one walked along were like the approaches to some as yet invisible Temple.

There are certain pictures of Jean Francois Millet's in which this quality of sanctity is the first thing that strikes one, the more so that the obviously religious element is conspicuously absent from them. His "Angelus" has always seemed to me a poorer composition in this respect than some others. When one sees a man standing with his hat off in the middle of a field, in the company of a woman, who clasps her hands, and looks down, one knows what one is expected to feel. When on the other hand one sees only a childish-looking farm-drudge knitting, a number of greedy sheep feeding, and a rough dog watching them, where, one asks oneself in perplexity, does the religious element come in? That it is to be found in the " Bergère " is however, unmistakable, and equally unmistakably was it to be found in the copse this morning, though how it got there, or who implanted it, I were rash were I to attempt to explain.

Assuredly man is by nature a devotional creature, however little of the dogmatic may mingle with his devotions. He may avert his ear from the church-going bell, he may refuse to label himself with the label of any particular denomination, but it is only to be overtaken with awe in the heart of a forest, and to fall on his knees, as it were, in some green secluded spot of the wilderness. The sense of something benignant close at hand, of some pitying eye surveying one, is so vivid at certain moments of one's life that it actually needs a rough conscious effort if one would shake it off. Even the sense of the vastness of that arena upon which our poor little drama is being played out, even this habitual impression becomes less grimly crushing at such moments than usual. What if it *is* colossal, one says to oneself, and what if, as compared to it, ourselves and our troubles *are* infinitesimal? what if they count no more in the scheme of things than do the afflictions of a broken-legged mouse, or of a crushed beetle? Very well; be it so. The mouse and the beetle have, after all, each their allotted place in that scheme. Nay for aught we know to the contrary, each may have its own incalculable hour; each may be susceptible of the same profound, if intangible, consolation.

JUNE 2, 1900

THE revolving year has brought us back at last to June. Here is June, and here are all the June flowers. If June were only always really June, and if our hearts could always keep time to its weather, then were earth paradise, and any remoter one might be relegated to the remotest of Greek kalends. June however is by no means invariably June, while as for our hearts they are like our eyes, which have a fashion of blinking sometimes at the light, as those of owls are reported to do, preferring their own shadowy places, and the night, which at least brings kindly dreams. Yet are kindly dreams, it may be asked, really the kindliest, seeing that we wake from them, and know that they are false? Are not ugly dreams, are not even terrible ones, better, seeing that we wake from them, and say to ourselves that matters, after all, are not quite so bad as *that*? It is a question, and, like many questions, a good deal easier asked than answered.

> " If there were dreams to sell,
> Pleasant, and sad as well,
> And the crier rang his bell,
> Which would you buy ? "

It is not the time, however, now for dreams, or for dream thoughts. It is nine o'clock in the morning, and everybody ought therefore to be wide awake and smiling. The garden at all events is performing its duty in both these respects, and seems, moreover, to be making encouraging little signals, like some humble but rather impatient suitor, who wishes to observe that he has really been waiting a long time, and deserves a little attention. Perhaps it does. Perhaps, seeing that it is there, and that we are here, it ought not to fare worse at our hands than our own dull bodies, which have to be clothed and fed, put to bed, and taken up again, whatever the less material portion may be feeling at the time. Here on my table I see is a list of some of our latest seedlings. They are not alpines this time, only common border plants, with a sprinkling of candidates for naturalisation, of which this copse can absorb almost any amount, so long as they are of the right sort. It is not a long list, and will not therefore take very long to transcribe.

Here it is :—

Adonis vernalis.
   ,,   pyrenaica.
Alströmeria aurantiaca.
Anchusa italica.
Anthemis tinctoria.
Aponogeton (self-sown).
Armeria cephalotes.
   ,,   ,,   alba.
Aster amellus.
   ,,   ericoides.
Campanula pyramidalis.
Catananche cærulea.
Commelina cælestis.
Chionodoxa sardensis.
Cimicifuga fœtida.
Chelone (Penstemon) barbata.
Clematis graveolens.
Cobæa scandens.
Convolvulus sylvatica.
Coreopsis lanceolata.
   ,,   tenuifolia.
Cistus laurifolius.
   ,,   formosus.
Cyclamen Coum.
   ,,   europæum.
   ,,   hederæfolium.
Cytisus scoparius.
   ,,   ,,   albus.
   ,,   Andreanus.

Cytisus præcox.
Delphinium (various).
Dictamnus fraxinella.
Dipsacus laciniatus.
Doronicum austriacum.
   ,,   plantaginum excelsum.
Eccremocarpus scaber.
Echinops Ritro.
   ,,   ruthenicus.
Erigeron speciosus.
Eryngium amethystinum.
   ,,   Olivierianum.
Onopordon arabicum.
   ,,   illyricum.
Ferula tingitana.
Francoa appendiculata.
Gaillardia grandiflora.
Gypsophila paniculata.
Heuchera sanguinea.
Hypericum calycinum.
   ,,   olympicum.
Iberis corifolia.
   ,,   sempervirens.
Lathyrus latifolius grandiflorus.
Lilium tigrinum (from bulblets in axils).
Lupinus arboreus.
   ,,   polyphyllus.

Lupinus polyphyllus alba.
Lythrum salicaria super-
    bum.
Libertia formosa.
Lobelia cardinalis.
Muscari armeniacum, } slow.
    „   conicum,
Meconopsis cambrica.
    „   nepalensis.

Meconopsis Wallichi.
Mimulus cardinalis.
Myosotis dissitiflora.
    „   sylvatica.
    „   palustris semper-
        florens.

.   .   .   .   .

.   .   .   .   .

My list appears to be a longer one than I
thought. I have as yet only reached the N's,
yet my energies have quite come to an end for
the present. I will put off the remainder of it
therefore for a day or two.

JUNE 8, 1900

I HAD intended going doggedly on this morning with the list of our seed-sowings, but another impulse has come, and the sowings must stand over for the moment.   Something in the look of to-day's sky and earth—a brand new earth after last night's rain—has brought a new, and a most unlooked-for wave of exhilaration to my mental shores, and the visitation is just now too rare and comforting not to be met half way with the keenest of hospitality.

"Life is a flux of moods," and to the fluctuations of those moods there is assuredly no limit. If we are eternally surprised by our own limitations, our own torpidity and dullness, there are also—and for this heaven be thanked—some possibilities of surprise upon the other side, and that for the oldest, the saddest, the least alert amongst us.   A hundred hours of intolerable dullness and stagnation pass over our heads. Then comes the hundred and first, and lo! the dull brain wakes, and the deaf ear hears. A new perception of the unperceived relationship of things ; a new perception of the invisible splendours lying unnoticed around us, becomes for the moment almost startlingly visible. Such hours are the only really countable ones, the chief solace of existence, the one clear reason, one is tempted to say, of our poor encumbered, stunted little lives. For their sakes, if for no other reason, it were well worth the trouble of being born, and of all the aches and ills that belong to that very singular estate ; worth our meeting gallantly, if possible merrily, the thousand petty pinpricks, the slings and arrows of outrageous fortune, the occasional alienation of those one loves best, nay—if it must be so— even the fell assaults of Giant Despair and all his abominable brood.

For the suggestiveness of what lies about us is no mere fancy, but is absolutely real ; real as the light upon yonder tree-tops ; real as the sorrow in our hearts ; real as the love that makes all things endurable ; real as the death which puts an end to pain. At this very moment, now passing over my head, there is lying about me— close to my eyes, could I but discern it—the materials alike of the loftiest poetry, and of the most riddle-solving science. Disregarded and unheeded there they lie, ready alike for the greatest singer in his happiest mood, for the

most era-making of discoverers, nay, for aught
I can tell to the contrary, for the seer, the saint,
and the prophet in their hours of highest, and
most God-inspired contemplation.

For the raw materials of inspiration are eternally
at hand, only invisibly. They are as present here
this morning as they ever were; present in the
earth and its green things; in the common
face of day; in the comings and goings of the
clouds, and of men; in the changes of the sky,
and of our own poor lives. The light that is
gilding yonder cumulus is as capable of inspiring
great thoughts here to-day in a Surrey copse, as
ever it was in Delphi, or in Argos, or in Jeru-
salem. It may awaken just as resounding
emotions, it may inspire just as great deeds to
the hearts of yonder passers-by in a dogcart, as
it did to the Assailants of Troy, or to the Seekers
of the Golden Fleece. The constituents of all
greatness, of all poetry, heroism, and sanctity
are for ever amongst us. It is only the right
recipients of them that are alas! so scanty.

And yet, even though we are not quite the
right recipients, it is well for us that such gleams
come. Who shall say that an existence which is
capable of being even thus temporarily lifted above
itself is not for that very reason a goodly and a
desirable one? What proportion of discomfort,
what proportion even of sheer pain, of numbing
weakness, of crushing sorrow were not worth

enduring so long as one knew—knew as a matter
of absolute certainty—that they would be now
and again pierced by gleams of such celestial
potency? The hard thing, and the thing that
for all mortals will always be hardest to bear
patiently, is—not the uncertainty even—so much
as the desperate transitoriness of such visitations. Almost before we have time to see and
to confer with them, our enchanting visitors
have spread out their gauzy wings, and have
vanished beyond recall. They are gone, but
where they are gone to, or when they will next
revisit us we have not the faintest notion. Ariel
and Titania have disappeared into the abyss, but
Caliban and Bottom on the contrary remain permanently behind, and are continually at our
elbows. At this very moment, and while I am
still thinking about it, the light is shifting rapidly.
The day has grown older; more crowded. A
thousand bloated nothings have sprung up like
so many fungi in the path. Shadows, slight,
but impenetrable, have gathered over the foreground. My own mood too has shifted, and
what a while ago seemed so clear has grown
fainter and fainter, and seems to be upon the
point of disappearing altogether. The good
little hour has passed!

JULY 7, 1900

ONCE more the great outside tide of life has beaten down the little barricades that one erects against it, and has come thundering in over them in an avalanche, tossing them to right and left, as though they were so many straws in its path! This week that has just ended has been for millions—for all Europe, for the whole world in fact—stamped with the impress of what one would fain still hope to be an incredible horror. Personally this Pekin nightmare has centred itself for me in the fact that E. B. was reported to be still there. Recently she was known to have been there, and whether she had, or had not left seemed at first impossible to ascertain. At last, though not until after days of suspense, of uncertainty, of growing hopelessness, came the telegram—"Safe at Hong Kong," and the relief is greater than it is easy, without exaggeration, to put into words.

So great has been that relief that for me it has perceptibly altered the whole situation, as I

suppose it was inevitable that it should do. Nevertheless, the tragedy as a tragedy remains, and if
anything seems to be deepening daily. The
newspapers certainly do nothing to minimise it;
perhaps they would say that it was hardly their
province to do so! Such headings, however, as
" The Chinese Cawnpore!" " Last shots reserved
for the women!" "White children carried on
spears!" seem to be rather more than it is their
absolute duty to offer to their readers! As
regards hope, no one appears to have any left, so
that it seems mere optimism to cherish any. A
ray reached us two days ago from our neighbour
S. B., who had heard of a reassuring telegram
from someone in Sir R. Hart's employment in
Pekin. No such gleam, however, seems to have
travelled down to the murky depths of our newspapers, so that one can only fear that there must
be some mistake.

It is with a sort of angry helplessness, mixed
with an instinctive feeling of self-defence, that
one turns from such accumulated, such carefully
elaborated horrors, and tries to forget them
in whatever little pursuit happens to lie nearest
to one's hand. It is not particularly creditable
to one's humanity that one should succeed in
doing so, and there is no denying that one's
attitude is essentially that of a kitten, or other
small Unreasonable, which runs after its ball,
though disaster may be hovering, or conflagration

about to involve, it and everyone else. Happily, we are made so, just as surely as the kitten is so made. We catch at straws, and in nine cases out of ten the straw saves us. Were it not for this same blessed prerogative of being interested in trifles, what, one sometimes asks oneself, would become of all our poor wits? or where on a journey so full of loss and sorrow, shock and trouble, would they have got to before the final goal is reached?

P

JULY 14, 1900

WITH a mind full of China, and its abomina-
tions, I happened this afternoon to take
up *The Opium Eater*, and opened full upon the
passages describing the results of the Malay's
visit. What imagery to be sure! What an
amazing rhetorician! Certainly if all life were
the feverish dream, the half nightmare, one is
tempted sometimes to call it, no greater exponent
of its terrors has ever existed than Thomas de
Quincey. Take this as a prelude.

"The Malay has been a frightful enemy for
months. I have been every night, through his
means, transported into Asiatic scenes. I know
not whether others share my feelings on this
point, but I have often thought that if I were
compelled to forego England, and to live in
China, and among Chinese manners, and modes
of life and scenery I should go mad. The causes
of my horror lie deep, and some of them must
be common to others. Southern Asia in general
is the seat of awful images and associations. As

the cradle of the human race it would alone have
a dim and reverential feeling connected with it.
But there are other reasons. . . . The mere
antiquity of Asiatic things, of their institutions,
histories, modes of faith, etc., is so impressive,
that to me the vast age of the race and name
overpowers the sense of youth in the individual.
A young Chinese seems to me an antediluvian
man renewed. . . . It contributes much to these
feelings that Southern Asia is and has been for
thousands of years, the part of the earth most
swarming with human life. The great *officina
gentium.* Man is a weed in these regions. The
vast empires into which the enormous population
of Asia has always been cast, give a further
sublimity to the feelings associated with all
Oriental names and images. In China, over
and above what it has in common with the rest
of Southern Asia, I am terrified by the modes
of life, by the manners, and the barrier of utter
abhorrence and want of sympathy, placed between us by feelings deeper than I can analyse.
I could sooner live with lunatics, or brute
animals."

Now for the dream proper.

" Under the connecting feeling of tropical heat
and vertical sunlights, I brought together all
creatures, birds, beasts, reptiles, all trees and
plants, usages and appearances, that are found
in all tropical regions, and assembled them

together in China, or Indostan. From kindred feelings I soon brought Egypt and all her gods under the same law. I was stared at, grinned at, hooted at, chattered at, by monkeys, by paraquets, by cockatoos. I ran into pagodas; and was fixed for centuries at the summit, or in secret rooms; I was the idol; I was the priest; I was worshipped; I was sacrificed; I fled from the wrath of Brahma through all the forests of Asia : Vishnu hated me; Seeva laid wait for me. I came suddenly upon Isis and Osiris; I had done a deed, they said, which the ibis and the crocodile trembled at. I was buried for a thousand years in stone coffins, with mummies and sphinxes, in narrow chambers, at the heart of eternal pyramids. I was kissed with cancerous kisses by crocodiles, and laid, confounded with all unutterable slimy things, amongst reeds and Nilotic mud."

JULY 28, 1900

THE last ten or twelve days have been different from any that I ever remember before. Circumstances have made them so, yet it has seemed as though there were something about themselves that has, as it were, affected those circumstances. For one thing it has been extraordinarily hot, so that we have been thankful for every breath of air that has travelled to us across the downs. The new little water-lily pond has been most kindly, and has contrived to produce an amazing illusion of coolness, while the oaks in whose shadow it lies have provided us with the reality of shade. We two have sat day after day for hours beside it, and the minutes have slipped along, like bubbles upon some very slow stream. There is a strange sense of unreality over everything ; a sense that everything is very near its end. The hours of a summer's day, and the years of a man's life seem to be much the same thing, and the one hardly longer than the other. The chimes from the clock across the valley are almost the only sounds that break in upon our stillness, for the birds sing very little just now. It has been a most strange fortnight; curiously unreal; extraordinarily dreamy and spectral-like. One by one its days have slipped by, very, very slowly, yet now that they are almost gone I say to myself— " How terribly swiftly ! "

THERE are times—surely we all know them
—when the injustices of life, of the individual destiny, seem more than can be silently
endured. "Why should this? and this? and
this be?" we ask. To what end such superfluous
happiness heaped upon one head, such equally
uncalled-for refusals of it consigned to another?
What does it mean? or who is the better for
such unendurable partiality?"

The question is the oldest of all questions,
yet it is the question of to-day, as it will be
the question of to-morrow, and of many more
to-morrows. Job asked it about himself, as
some of us ask it about those whom we know
to be infinitely better than ourselves. Moreover it is not alone the apparent injustice of a
life as a whole, but of the several parts of it,
that we murmur at. There are acts of courage,
of silent endurance, of unrecognised heroism,
which only need to be performed in some more
conspicuous fashion, or upon a larger field, to

awaken the whole world to admiration. Yet
they pass away unnoticed; oblivion enshrouds
them, and they are never so much as heard of.

When such suppressions, such seeming injustices, occur at the beginning of things, while
the sun is still high, and Time seems a friendly
factor, one is able to reassure oneself. One
says—"Wait a little longer!" "The time will
come!" When such illusion, however, is no
longer possible; when the sands have run out,
or been scattered in mid-career; what is one to
say *then*? What faith, what philosophy, what
stoicism, or what mixture of all three, will enable
one to accept it without complaint?

AUGUST 4, 1900

OF the vicissitudes of this year there seem to be no end! After we have mourned over these victims of Pekin as men mourn over those for whom there is absolutely no hope; after we have enumerated their names, like the names upon a death-roll, and all but held a national funeral service in their memory; and after we have followed their last moments; gloried in its heroism; wept over its tragedy; starved, sighed, bled, almost died with them; lo, it appeareth now that none of them are dead at all! Was ever an entire continent in the history of the world so mercilessly defrauded before of its tears?

I have no notion how they may feel about it themselves, but my impression is that were I the responsible head of a daily newspaper I should prefer to immure myself from society for the next few days! There is a pile of such papers at this moment in my sanctum, which I have just been turning over, and reading a few of the head-lines with some little inward entertainment. Not that I pretend for a moment to have been one whit wiser, or less lugubrious myself! Far from it. We have all been a flight of ravens and screech-owls together, only that some of us have screeched and flapped our wings a little more energetically, and in rather a more public fashion than the rest!

FEW of the minor experiences of life are, I think, more consoling than to come across some small link in the chain of natural law, over the right connections of which one has long groped blindly. Such a little bit of good luck befell me only yesterday. In itself it was what one calls the veriest trifle; simply a question as to the relationship of certain obscure organisms, profoundly uninteresting to the world at large. To myself it seemed, for a while at all events, to be of some little consequence. It imparted—for fully ten minutes—an entirely new impression of a vast, a peaceful, and a most orderly progress. It seemed to open up vistas into the perfection, into the breadth, no less than the complexity, of that great scheme of Life, of which we ourselves form a part. It came as a sudden vision, as a conception of possibilities—I hardly know what to call it—the vividness of which it would be difficult without exaggeration to put into words.

For those who, like myself, are the mere irre-
sponsible camp-followers of science, the importance of any given solution seems often to be
less in what it actually teaches us, than in what
it allows us indirectly to guess at. The new fact
may or may not be important, but the ideas that
it starts in our minds can hardly fail to be so.
In the imaginative realm there is literally no limit
to the revelations to which the tiniest of natural
phenomena may not serve as an introduction.
The fact itself may be the minutest of facts; a
mere pin-point, a scarce perceptible chink of light,
but it is a chink in the walls as it were of a great
cathedral of discovery, the doors of which may,
for anything one knows to the contrary, be
thrown widely open to oneself, and to everyone
else to-morrow.

This, if I am not misleading myself, is the real
attractiveness of every pursuit which has the
elucidation of Nature for its end and aim; one
perhaps most felt, or at all events most enjoyed,
by the more ignorant of her votaries. Properly
directed ignorance is in truth a most desirable
haze, and when some stray beam does traverse
its obscurity, how great is the illumination which
follows! What may not be possible where there
is no dead-weight of fact to keep our feet upon
the solid earth; no panoply of unescapable
knowledge to bid our pleasant fancies nay?

Even for those less comfortably unfettered

by circumstances, it must be an alleviation surely of the prose of life that in this region of the ideas no man can ever positively say what may not be in store for him. However tame, however dull his foreground, there is always the chance of something ahead ; something that when it comes, will sweep his thoughts away with it to the very verge of the horizon. There is never a day, there is hardly an hour, in which some new idea may not be upon its road. Now a really new idea for the time being remakes life. It is a solvent which dissolves all old impressions, and rebuilds them anew. Men live by ideas, as surely, almost as literally, as they live by bread, and a world into which no new idea ever entered would be a dead world, tenanted only by corpses.

The strange thing is that we should any of us doubt this, or that in those innermost citadels which we call our brains, we should really very greatly care about anything else. Surely for people so oddly circumstanced as ourselves the quest for ideas, ever larger, ever more comprehensive ideas, is the only perfectly rational occupation ? Stranded upon the shores of the Unknown ; rocked to and fro by all the winds of mystery ; ignorant of whence precisely we came, whither precisely we are going ; for people in so strange a position as this to be continually on the quest for some new intimation, for some further hint, or indication, seems as natural as for shipwrecked sailors to be for ever on the watch for sails.

I remember—it is years since, yet the impression is as clear as though it were yesterday —one who, during the vigils of a sleepless night, slipped suddenly into a dream. And in that dream it seemed to the dreamer as though he stood upon a narrow-topped hill, encompassed by all the stars, and lifted high in air above the slumbering earth. And, looking upwards, he was aware of a sky, immeasurably vaster and higher, or so he thought, than he had ever observed any sky to be before. And, still gazing into that vast sky, the dreamer perceived that it was filled with what at first he took to be snowflakes. Looking more closely he saw that, if snowflakes, then they were snowflakes lit up by all the colours of the prism. And one of these snowflakes, just then slowly descending, touched the dreamer's head with a soft, but quite a sensible impact. And as it touched him, lo, a new thought sprang up, alive, full-fledged, wonderful, within his brain ; a thought absolutely unsuspected by him before ; vast, formative, irresistible, like some new law of Evolution, or of Gravitation. And, with it, light seemed to break in upon him from every side at once, and a great joy, and a sense of elasticity such as he had never known before. And a voice said—

" These are the thoughts with which this earth
of yours has been built up, and all yonder other
earths, of which this is one of the very least."
And another voice said—" They are as the sands
of the sea for multitude, and of the secrets
hidden in them, and of the wonder, and satisfaction, and delight of those secrets there is no
end."

Then that sleeper awoke, and, though the
night was still long and dark, the thought of
his dream remained with him, and was like the
song of a thrush in his heart until the morning.

AUGUST 10, 1900

LIFE; Life the indomitable, the multifarious;
Life, as it rises in the scale, becoming conscious of itself—the thought of this recurs again
and again to one's mind, and each time with a
greater sense of power, and of a sort of consolation. What limit need be assigned, one asks
oneself, to its capabilities, to the endless trans-
formations, to the possibilities, as yet unguessed
at, which may have been destined for it by its
Inventor from the beginning of things? If the
mere personal consciousness, the precarious personal life, is rarely without an element of discomfort, in this larger sense that personal life all
but disappears, and with the loss of it comes—
not perhaps actual joy, that could hardly be
looked for—but at least a great exhilaration,
an extraordinary sense of width, of serenity,
and of detachment.

As the mind descends deeper and deeper into
that serene abyss it seems to shake itself free for
the time being from all that confused, battling,

disturbing sea in which its daily lot is cast. As that downward course continues, all that appertains to the surface becomes more and more dreamlike, as it might to a diver, and the mind widens and strengthens insensibly with each descending fathom. "Life" is indeed a marvellous shibboleth; a spell that unlocks innumerable doors; a word of varied and manifold meanings. Merely to write it down, merely to utter it, seems to clear the atmosphere. Mental fogs of all kinds at that touch roll up their dingy tents, and depart. An impression of morning—fresh, imperishable morning—hovers around it; youth, health, fecundity, vigour belong to it. All the winds of Spring—"driving sweet buds, like flocks to feed in air"—rush after it, and fan it on its course. The sense of the good green earth, and of all those good green things that belong to it, pours in a stream of joy through even the dreariest veins. "And if one little planet is able to show it in this inexhaustible profusion, what of all the other planets?" one thinks. "What of those countless other worlds, all belonging to the same great plan; all built and upheld by the same architectonic hand; all strung, as it were, upon one great string, and vibrating eternally to a single immortal touch?"

Q

AUGUST 18, 1900

STANDING, shortly after dusk yesterday evening, upon the edge of the slope which drops suddenly into the valley enclosing our village and its church, my ear was filled with a variety of sounds, all of them familiar, yet none somehow quite recognisable; all with a certain strangeness about them, born no doubt of the mist and of the oncoming obscurity.

Sounds which reach our ears after nightfall never seem to be quite the same sounds as in the daytime, even though they may be produced by exactly the same means. Commonplace in reality, they are never perfectly commonplace in their effect. They awaken curious echoes. They bring back odd, and half-vanished thoughts. They play the same rather uncanny tricks with the brain as they doubtless did in the days of the Patriarchs, or of the Shepherd Kings. The bark of a dog half a mile away will conjure up visions of hunting scenes, swift and phantasmagoric as the pageant of a dream. The sharp " click-clack " of a horse's hoof; the crunching of a waggon-wheel; most of all, perhaps, the

thin, lamentable, bleating of sheep floating up
from the valley; all these set vibrating fibres
within us which have their roots as far back in
the history of the race as anything well can be.
Our life of to-day, with all its crowded impedi-
menta, tends at such moments to sink suddenly,
and to disappear. We realise—if only during
the duration of a lightning flash—that we are
standing, not in the least upon any apex, merely
upon some small peak on one of the sides of the
great organic mountain. That we are looking
at a scene which has witnessed the arrival of
our race, as of other races, upon it, and which
will assuredly one day witness its departure again.
That all that we can discern is but, as it were, a
few front streaks upon the surface of an ocean,
rolling on without bourne or limit. And at that
realisation the mind is apt to start, and to shiver
instinctively, as before some yawning gulf, opening
unexpectedly below the feet.

Such little mental peaks afford, in truth, but
a dizzy standing ground, and are best, perhaps
for that reason, not ascended too often. Just as
the trade of the astronomer is said to need a
sound leaven of stolidity before it can be safely
embarked upon, so only a very strong head can
with safety peer long into a void, hardly less
perturbing and intoxicating than that into which
it is his business to pry. Those capricious little
particles, upon which all our comfort depends,

dislike it, and they are probably right in doing so. It is true that what we call the Past, that which is entirely put away, and done with, might seem to be a harmless enough subject of contemplation. So conceivably it might be, were it not for the fact that in following it one is apt to find oneself brought suddenly face to face with the other, and the far more formidable brother; the one whose kingdom lies, not behind us, but ahead. At those dim barriers all real advance is inexorably stayed; into the recesses beyond them no secular lantern has ever peered; while even our most authoritative, our most convinced guides, can at best assure us as to its geography with hesitating, and often curiously conflicting voices.

To abstain from all attempts at peering into that obscurity is more perhaps than can be asked of mortals. The less of such peerings we indulge in, however, surely the better, because the saner, because, also, the more trustful. Of all the cataracts of words, poured in verbal Niagaras over this momentous topic, have there been many, I wonder, wiser or truer than these of old Hooker? I write them down as they have lodged in my memory; probably therefore quite incorrectly.

"Rash were it for the feeble mind of man to wade far into the doings of the Almighty. For though 'tis Joy to know Him, and Pride to make mention of His name, yet our deepest Wisdom is to know that we know Him not, and our truest Homage is our Silence."

AUGUST 25, 1900

FROM gropings along unlit ways, and towards an undiscoverable goal, what a pleasant experience it is to turn suddenly back to the well-trodden paths of a near and a tried companionship! It is almost an exact parallel to the sensations of the child who, having rushed out of its home into the wild winter night, full of hollow reverberations, and perturbing gleams, suddenly retreats, and finds itself once more beside the hearth, with an absolutely new sense of its security, and wide-armed delightfulness.

Upon few topics has more ink been expended than upon this one of friendship. As regards one point all the pens have I think been agreed, and that is that diversity constitutes its soundest basis. If a truism, this is at least one of those truisms that every day's experience throws into new relief. Friendship demands absolutely no conformity, but lives, thrives, and has its being upon the most absolutely radical differences. Friend and friend may differ by nearly everything that can differentiate one human being from another. By the tenour of their thoughts; by the circumstances of their lives; by the very texture of their brains, their souls, their hearts, their entire natures. Friendship makes light of such little discrepancies as these. Its roots push down to a stratum where even the largest of them become mere accidents, and at that serene depth they meet and lock securely under them all.

To say that such a tie is the great ameliorator of life, the soother of its sorrows, the encourager of its brighter moments, is to say ridiculously little. To say that it is one that we could hardly endure to think of existing without, is to say almost less. The very notion of such a deprivation produces a sort of vertigo; a species of mental confusion, akin to the thought of losing identity itself. Worse, indeed, for it is not merely the everyday, the vulgar self, that such a loss— supposing it to be complete—would deprive one of. It is that other, better, and more shining self, which only really exists inside the enchanted walls of a loving, sympathetic friendship. Within those fostering walls it grows, expands, and flourishes, but outside of them it sickens, pines away, and dies.

It is a very singular tie, when one reflects a little upon it; so close often that no nearness of blood, no identity of name, could, so far as one can see, make it any closer. It seems to be antecedent, not alone to itself, but to the whole social warp and woof, of which it is an outcome. Just as the trees in one wood seem, to anyone who wanders often in it, to have acquired a sort of identity, so two who have walked for some time very closely together, though they may differ as widely as an ash does from a pine, as an oak does from a hornbeam, acquire a sort of similarity, due to the same sunshine having warmed, the same storms having shaken and darkened both. It is well to speak a good word now and then of a personage whom one habitually abuses, so let it be recorded in favour of that odd compound of good and ill which we call our existence that, if it has thwarted our desires, dwarfed our ambitions, nipped in our joys, chilled back our aspirations, cut down our hopes, and not infrequently wrung our hearts, at least——it has given us our friends!

SEPTEMBER 4, 1900

SURELY people live fast in these days, even the very slowest of them! I find myself turning back of a morning to the thoughts of the Transvaal, and of the struggle still going on there, with the oddest sense of renewal; as of one trying to rekindle dead fires, or to reawaken some set of well-nigh obliterated emotions. When did it begin, this war, which seems to have been going on throughout the greater part of one's lifetime? which the newspapers have again and again announced to be just over, but with which they nevertheless manage to fill several columns every morning? It is perhaps a mere personal impression, due to closer anxieties, but to myself the fears and perturbations of last spring seem often almost incredibly remote. There are moments when they appear to be as out of date for any practical purpose as the alarms that convulsed our grandfathers and grandmothers two generations ago. *E pur si muove!* It is still going on, this war of ours, and seems likely moreover, to do so for a considerable time longer. Botha, De Wet, Delarey, with half a dozen more guerrilla leaders, are swarming about, active as ants, and at least as dangerous as hornets. We have got Pretoria, but we have emphatically *not* got our new colonies, though both, I see, are now officially annexed. That we shall get them some day or other, and that the last of England's big daughters will—in the course, say of the coming century—become as friendly and tolerant of her as are the other two, a good many people seem to expect. Possibly. The very moderate view she takes of the motherly function will certainly be a help in that direction. In these days grown-up daughters are not expected fortunately to be deferential—especially, perhaps, to their mothers.

The closing scenes of a war have a tendency to awaken in some speculative minds thoughts of war as a whole; of the entire attitude of man as a combative being. So long as the particular struggle we have been watching remains at the acute stage, so long especially as the faintest doubt exists as to its final result, such a merely academic attitude is impossible. Pride; dignity; honour; fear of what may be; anger, perhaps, at what has been; all these rush in a tide through even the most tepid veins, and everything else is for the time being as though it were not. When however the struggle is nearing its

end ; when the trumpets are beginning to sound
the recall, and the fighting, even if it still goes
on, appears on both sides to be growing somewhat perfunctory ; then thoughts of what it
all means, thoughts of War in the abstract,
make themselves felt, and in place of hanging
breathlessly over the newspapers, one wonders,
as one saunters to and fro the garden, whether
this same instinct of combativeness really is an
integral part of man's nature ?   Whether, in
other words, it is an absolutely incurable disease,
congenital to the species, or merely a sort of
youthful malady, destined, like other youthful
maladies, to pass away, as a very slowly evolv-
ing race attains nearer and nearer to its full
maturity ?

In a year when the roll and rumble of cannon
have never ceased even for a day; when the rattle
of rifle-shot has seemed like something that had
become part of every brain ; when all public
life has centred round a single point, and the
most reticent of races has flung its reticence
utterly to the winds ; in such a year so remote
and speculative a fashion of looking at the matter
strikes even the speculator himself as somewhat
thin, and cold-blooded.   "What right," he turns
round, and asks himself hotly, "what right have
you, or such as you, people who, far from taking
any part in the struggle, have kept out of even
the very wind and whiff of it!   Who have char-

tered no yachts, nursed no wounded, sung no war songs, or even—lowest of all the efforts of patriotism—so much as composed any! Who have remained at home the whole time; tending your own gardens, culling your own fancies, and sorrowing over your own sorrows. What right have such as you—idlers, cumberers, that you are!—so much as to mention the word "war" at all?

"Very true," the other self answers submissively. And yet again, he reflects, as he looks around him, is it not, after all, just such little plots as these that the earthquake of battle has this year shaken the most fiercely? Is it not such gardens as these—not this one perhaps, but others almost identical; flowery places, where the robins peck about, and where no hostile foot has ever trod—is it not against these that the harshest blows have been struck, where the cruellest wounds have been received? Quick, quick, as in a dream, fancy conjures up a vision —a procession, rather—floating along upon the soft bands of autumn sunshine; a procession of mothers, of sisters, of betrothed ones, of wives. As each in turn passes by memory evokes the face, or the faces, that belong to it; then turns to linger last and longest with the mothers. Ah, those mothers! God's pity, above all others, rest this year with the mothers. For whom hope can never be anything again but a delusive word; for whom the future can hold *no* compensations ; for whom the very things that they love the best— their gardens ; the walks they pace along ; the flowers that they stoop to pick—must henceforth seem all bestreaked and shadowed over by the red, abhorrent shadow of the battlefield. Truly the garden is a place of peace, but it may also be a place of the most cruel, the most unde- served war, and the bullets that have been speed- ing thousands of miles away, have too often found their last, and their deadliest targets within its circle.

SEPTEMBER 10, 1900

THE year has more than run its complete round
since these loosely connected jottings were
begun, so that it is high time that they shut the
cover down upon themselves, and withdrew into
a corner. Diary-keeping, like knitting, like whit-
tling, like any other of the minor distractions,
begins often with more or less effort, yet after
a time becomes, first a habit, finally almost a
necessity. Entered upon without any particular
motive, it creates a place for itself, it fills a
void, it becomes a solace. The practice of the
diarist varies, of course, almost infinitely. It may
mean merely that conscientious daily record, to
which alone the words "journal," "diary," "day-
book" properly belong, or it may enlarge its
scope until it covers all those looser, and neces-
arily more intermittent outpourings, in which
most of us from time to time indulge, whether
for our weal or our woe depends largely upon
circumstances.

One merit it certainly has. Few mediums of

thought are equally fluid; few admit of greater variety; more diversity of mood; more ranging from topic to topic. Possibly the most satisfactory of all its developments is when it enables us to follow some well-beloved pursuit, keeping pace with its minutest ramifications, losing ourselves, as it were, in its existence, and thereby evading half those irritating points, half those wounding asperities that belong to every human lot. Amongst such beloved and healing pursuits that of gardening stands prominently forward. I have been assured that there are superior persons by whom it is held in exceedingly low repute; who regard it as a symptom, indeed, of mental degeneration, and, as a resource, below stamp-collecting, and about on a par with the acquisition of the idiot stitch. Were it my lot to be acquainted with any such superior persons there is one punishment that I must confess I should dearly love to bestow upon them; which is that they should first desperately need the comfort of such a solace, and afterwards—upon due probation and penitence—that they should come to find it! Few ideas are more bigoted, more essentially narrow and foolish, than this one about the elevating, or the non-elevating effect of our pursuits. It is upon a par with the equally pestilent notion that it is the narrowness of our lives, or the obscurity of our lots, that keeps our swelling souls from greatness. Greatness, like genius, is dependent upon no such trumpery circumstances, but is a self-existent quality, not to be concealed though it were hidden under all the rocks of Mount Ararat, or had every wave in the Atlantic piled upon its head. Let us then assert, roundly assert, that no pursuit — certainly no natural pursuit—can with any accuracy be called petty. It is, moreover, the great advantage of all such out-of-door pursuits that they enable their followers to confer with Nature at first hand, and not through any intermediary. This is recognised in the case of what are called the higher natural pursuits, but it is equally true of all. Like many other potentates Nature has her unpleasant, even her very dangerous aspects, but it is one of her best points that she is no respecter of persons. She is an autocrat, and an autocrat in whose eyes all subjects stand upon precisely the same level. At her court there is no superior, and no inferior. Geologist, botanist, zoologist, horticulturist—beetle-hunter, stone-breaker, weed-picker, crab-catcher—it matters not what we call ourselves, or what others call us, so long as it is herself alone we follow, she receives us all alike. Within those imperial and open-doored halls of hers all rapidly find their own level; all may speak to her on occasion face to face; all present their own credentials, and all are accepted by her with the same serene, the same absolutely indifferent toleration.

It is not even as if her greater secrets were reserved for the wiser and the more erudite of her followers, and were withheld from those that were less erudite, for the same partial revelations, the same profound concealments, seem, so far as can be ascertained, to be allotted to all alike. The Sphinx which looks up out of the heart of a toadflax or a columbine is the same Sphinx that speaks out of the stilly night, out of the clouds, out of the primæval rocks, out of the stars, and out of the inviolable sea. "And this," she possibly murmurs, "is my lesson which I give to you. Cease to occupy yourself wholly with the shows of the surface, the toys of to-day; things which come and go, which pass and end in an hour. Look a little deeper. Follow any of these brown roots down to where the motherly earth receives them, and the dews and the rain nourish them, and all the complicated chemistry of my workshops have been at work from the beginning to bring them to perfection. On and on, deeper and deeper yet, towards that vaster laboratory across whose threshold even I have never glanced. There, in that incredible remoteness, thou and I ; the small brown worm, and the goodly oak ; the old, worn-out worlds, and the new, as yet only half-born stars ; all the gay shows of this little green earth, and all the unknown things of the immeasurable Cosmos, meet, and are on a level. There is neither larger or smaller there, neither younger or older, neither wiser or more foolish, neither less or more important. For out of it came that by means of which all this that we see and know has come. There, once for all, was uttered that spell of which this huge teeming universe is but the outcome. There Life herself was born, and it may be therefore other powers, greater and more wide-embracing than even Life herself. But of what that spell consists, or what the name of it is, no bird, or beast, or man, or possibly other creature, has hitherto so much as even begun to guess."

R

SEPTEMBER 11, 1900

SO one ends. Yet, even in the very act of
ending, qualms arise. Thinking of what
lies under one's hand, no longer as a sheaf
of familiar manuscript, but as a full-blown book,
printed, bound, stitched, and a' the lave o' it,
misgivings awake, and are lively. Only yesterday I sounded the praises of the diary, and I
do so still; yet the manifest destiny of every
diary is to live a life of absolute seclusion, and,
when it has served its turn, to feed the fire. It
is true that one may murmur something to
oneself about "subjective"; "subjective forms
of literature," but the words ring hollow, and
have little validity. In a well-known passage
Carlyle has described a visit which he paid
to the Sage of Highgate, whom he found
sitting in his Dodona oak grove—otherwise
Mr. Gilman's house and garden—"as a kind of
Magus, girt in mystery and enigma." " I still
recollect," Carlyle says, "his ' object,' and ' subject,' and how he sang and snuffled them into

'om-m-mject' and 'sum-m-mject,' with a kind
of solemn shake or quaver, as he rolled along."
The diarist need not necessarily roll along, and
has no pretensions certainly to be called a sage,
yet he too is apt now and again to murmur
"sum-m-mject," "sum-m-mjective," with a sound
that even in his own ears rather resembles
that of some bumble-bee upon a summer's
morning; extremely self-important, that is to
say, but not particularly lucid. It is true that
so far as self-importance is concerned he stands
absolutely excused, seeing that egotism is his
profession. To cease to be egotistic is to cease
to be a diarist altogether. This is as clear as
it is satisfactory, but it can hardly be said to
meet the point. There is nothing odd, of course,
about a man or a woman being confidential with
himself or herself; it is when they proceed to
drop their confidences into other, and less in-
dulgent ears, that the oddity begins.

There are moreover seasons when such outpourings seem even less appropriate than others,
and this year—September to September—appears, looking back, to be one of these. It
has been a black, a despairingly black, twelve
months for thousands; how black, how despairing, few of those thousands would have credited
when it began. Amongst those incredulous ones,
though on somewhat different grounds, the diarist
might have been reckoned. Diary-keeping is

not entirely a matter of egotism and of intro-
spection, of fun, and of frolic, though it may
appear to the non-diarist to be.   What a nice
innocent-looking book it seems, when its spaces
are all blank, and the days they refer to are not
yet born! yet such a book may come to look
like a mere fragment of malicious destiny, bound
in calf or calico.   Holding it in his hands the
would-be diarist turns the leaves over one by
one with a smile.   How will this, and this, and
this space be filled up? he wonders.   What odd
little adventures will they have to record?   What
absurdities of his own, or of others, to recount?
What   books   read?   what   expeditions   made?
what   trees   or   shrubs   planted?   So   he   sets
jauntily forth on his self-appointed task, to be
met by——What?   A   thought   to   give   the
lightest pause.

    And yet, and yet.   Let the very worst come
to pass that can come to pass, even so an attitude of mere unmitigated despair hardly befits
fast disappearing mortals, whose breath is in
their nostrils.   Looking backwards may seem
all gloom and pain, and looking forward no
better, possibly rather worse, and yet assuredly
it is *not* all gloom, or all pain.   Enchanting
things spring up by thousands in the ugliest of
clefts, and the barest of trees may serve as a
perch for some winter-singing robin.   Sorrow
itself, carried out into the open air, under the

benignant arch of heaven, changes in some degree its character. It is Sorrow still, but it is Sorrow with a difference. It seems to merge into the category of other things ; terrible ones, it is true, but still natural—earthquakes, volcanoes, avalanches, pestilences, and so forth—things that we shrink from, but that we cannot reasonably resent. The sense of wrong, of hardship, of bitterness, of personal injustice, seems by degrees to melt away from it, and therefore it can be better faced. At least it is well that we should tell ourselves so.

THE END

For EU product safety concerns, contact us at Calle de José Abascal, 56–1°,
28003 Madrid, Spain or eugpsr@cambridge.org.